A Hard Chance

Sailing Into The Heart of Love

Tom Gallant

Pottersfield Press, Lawrencetown Beach, Nova Scotia, Canada

Library and Archives Canada Cataloguing in Publication

Gallant, Tom, 1946-
A hard chance : sailing into the heart of love / Tom Gallant.
ISBN 1-895900-68-9

1. Gallant, Tom, 1946- 2. Gallant, Melissa.
3. Brain -- Wounds and injuries -- Patients -- Nova Scotia – Biography.
4. Authors, Canadian (English) – Biography. I. Title.

RD594.G34 2005 362.19'7481044'092 C2005-900554-8

Front cover photo: David Pu'u

Author photo: Chris Reardon

Cover design: Tom Gallant, Lesley Choyce, Dalhousie Graphics

Editing: Julia Swan, Peggy Amirault, Lesley Choyce

Pottersfield Press acknowledges the ongoing support of The Canada Council for the Arts, as well as the Nova Scotia Department of Tourism, Culture and Heritage, Cultural Affairs Division. We also acknowledge the financial support of the Government of Canada through the Book Publishing Industry Development Program for our publishing activities.

Pottersfield Press
83 Leslie Road
East Lawrencetown
Nova Scotia, Canada, B2Z 1P8
Website: www.pottersfieldpress.com
To order, phone 1-800-NIMBUS9 (1-800-646-2879)
Printed in Canada

Canada Council for the Arts Conseil des Arts du Canada

For Melissa, that she might remember.

For Belinda, that she might know her father.

And for my father, my first best teacher.

I knew that topless lady had
something up her sleeve. – John Prine

Prologue

THREE TIMES I STARTED THIS BOOK, and three times I bailed out at around fifty pages. The reason was always the same. It didn't sound right. It was too sad, too happy, too proud, too humble. It was always wrong. But many who know me well had asked for this story and I knew damn well that I had to write it. I knew this because I knew that I had learned something here, something serious and true, and if that won't make a book, what will?

This is a story of a tragedy. But it isn't sad. Like humans do, when hurt beyond all reasonable measure, Melissa and I rose from the ashes and carried on. We did it day by day, week by week, year by year. The test life provided us was diabolical in its intensity and would become a relentless and lifelong presence. This is why, after all these years, I finally found a tone of voice I could live with and made one last try at telling the story.

Telling the story. Some strange accident of birth or experience has left me believing that stories are the best window on the truth that we have. I will walk past the philosophers and academics, scientists and experts of every stripe to get to the old fella in the corner who's spinning a yarn, every time. This has always been the case. I don't remember deciding one day that I loved storytellers and wanted to become one. As a fish born in the sea learns to swim without thinking about it, I was immersed in the business of storytelling from earliest memory. A story organizes and makes some sense out of the raw materials of experience.

The experiences I'm relating here were focused by one incident, one brutal intrusion on our lives that changed everything. It was unwished for and would be easy to see as the act of a cruel Creator. In fact, it's just what happened. Bad things happen all the time. Bad things are the meat and potatoes of storytelling. Somehow, the act of organizing all of it into this book was necessary, as necessary as eating good food, singing good songs, having good friends in your life.

The most difficult thing about all of this is that the story is true, it happened to us, and so I didn't have the protection that fiction provides. I had never intended to write a memoir or anything like it. I like taking things that happen and spinning them out into stories leavened by the unfettered workings of imagination and fancy. The playful aspect of inventing turns of plot, creating characters and settings is the fun that makes the hard work of writing worthwhile. Here, I was constantly aware of the shortcomings of memory, the impossibility of finding a truly objective point of view. When I lost faith in all of it, I turned to friends for help.

Early on in the writing, when there were only a few chapters done, I sent what I had written to Silver Donald Cameron, a friend and colleague for longer than either one of us cares to remember. He and Marjorie read what I had written and insisted that I continue in letters that I treasure still. Then, a little later, I sent five chapters to Lesley Choyce. He responded that he would publish the book. And he provided just what was needed. A deadline, and wise and gentle editorial guidance. His advice and confidence were crucial.

Occasionally, around the dinner table I would read a chapter or two to friends and they would listen with open hearts.

John Steele and Peg Greer were especially kind in this regard. And then there are the fellow travellers, those to whom I could talk in a more general and abstract way about the job at hand. My sister Catherine, who has published an exquisite memoir of her own (*The Brow of Dawn*), has always been and always will be the most caring and optimistic of soul mates. I treasure her beyond saying. We talked for hours about the problem of getting it down right, making it true.

William Gilkerson, a writer and artist of international reputation and a fellow sailor, was always there to commiserate when futility raised its head. We laughed about the elaborate foolishness of the writer skulking up to the blank page all full of fear and hope.

Stuart Margolin, the fine actor/director, is the kind of friend you thank the gods for, always wise to the dark side and driving towards the light. While we worked on a screenplay together, we talked about the books we were writing. There was comfort and inspiration there. My dear and essential friend, Bill Fleming, who was also in on the screenplay, provided some necessary notes, and even more necessary whimsy and humour. Julia Swan, my editor, provided precision, encouragement and good solid advice. This is exactly what an editor should do, and I was lucky to have her help.

And then there's Melissa, the hero of the book. As I wrote it, I would read it to her, a chapter at a time. She laughed and cried and when it was hard for her to listen to, she held her head up and toughed it out. None can know, myself included, how terrible it is to lose a large part of yourself forever, and yet to live. She bears this with dignity and courage and humour. Every book begins with inspiration. Some fall short of, some go far beyond, what brought them into being. In this case, no matter how the book is judged, the inspiration was Melissa.

1

SHE ALMOST DIED. If she had, my life would have been easier. I would have grieved the loss, and gone back to whatever it was I was doing, somehow better for it all. In time, I would have found another love, for the company of women is essential. But she didn't die, though the person who survived is someone else, someone other, who carries within haunting echoes of the lost one who was my wife.

She lived. Melissa Andrelle Groseclose lived and still I lost the wild brave beauty who could knock over any room she entered with a glance, and gained this strange creature, this aching heart, one good eye imploring, "Who am I?" I was given a guru, a teacher without a memory or an agenda, a soul forever locked in the here and now. Here is what happened.

There is a four-way intersection outside the impossibly quaint old town of Lunenburg, Nova Scotia. It is a difficult place, for there is a curve leading into it on the road from town that hides the oncoming traffic from those who would cross until it's just too late. Melissa and I were stopped at this intersection. It was the second of July, 1992. That much I remember.

She was driving. She looked one way, then the other and entered the intersection. We were hit in the driver's-side door by the Halifax to Bridgewater bus, driven ninety feet sideways – with the bus's brakes in lock. I remember none of this. It is said I got out of our van and staggered around crying for help for Melissa until I collapsed face first on the highway. It is said it took volunteer firemen using the Jaws of Life a half hour to extract Lissa from the van. I don't know. I don't remember.

I do remember waking up in the Fisherman's Memorial Hospital in Lunenburg and seeing the concerned faces of friends swimming before me. My t-shirt was torn and bloody, my leg hurt, everything hurt. I heard my voice, disembodied.

"What happened?"

"You had an accident."

"Where's Lissa?"

"The ambulance is taking her to Halifax."

"Is she all right?"

"It doesn't look good."

I remember this exchange because it happened a hundred times as I slipped in and out of consciousness. My friend Pete Tanner had been told by the doctor to keep me from going to sleep. I had a serious concussion, and the first few hours were crucial. So over and over again, he answered my questions, and over and over again I forgot the answers. The memory is a fragile thing. When struck from without, it goes away. Where does it go? I wish I knew.

The morning after the accident, I woke to pains more vivid than the night before. The shock was wearing away, and the reality of the situation was making its brutal self known.

I didn't want to know. I wanted more painkillers. I wanted painkillers for my aching body and my bruised heart and soul. I wanted it all to go away. It wouldn't. Grim-faced friends stood at my bedside and tried to find some hope, some humour. It's miraculous how we find friends and gather them into our lives. There's little in life that's more important, yet most of us have the wisdom to leave the getting of friends to chance.

Chance.

IN 1979 I WROTE A RADIO PLAY CALLED *A Jazz Lover.* It was full of the ache of lost love, a prophecy of my own soon-to-be broken heart. My love affair of seven years was breaking apart. I was in denial but the woman's eyes looked past me to a horizon we didn't share. By the time the play went to air on the CBC, she had her own apartment and I was living on my schooner. These were not desolate times. The schooner was new to me, a childhood dream coming true. A broken heart was just the thing to impart the necessary gravitas. My journal was turgid. I had tried hard to love that woman.

I liked the simple ritual of my days. I was tied up at Mader's Wharf in Mahone Bay, then a real wharf behind a real hardware store and warehouse. Each morning, I would wake, and after coffee, clamber up on the wharf and walk to the post office. On the morning in question, I received a card from an art gallery in Halifax. I slipped the card in my shoulder bag and continued to the liquor store where I bought a bottle of demerara. Then to the grocery store, and back to the schooner, the journal and my grand broken heart. It was spring, and the ice had left the bay.

I don't remember what I did with the afternoon that day. Probably worked at getting the boat ready for the sailing season. But the evening was cool, and I put a fire in the coal stove, a Lunenburg Foundry "gift," and made a pot of stew. As was my habit on the good days, I lit the kerosene lamps and a solitary candle on the table. I set a place for myself and ate with some ceremony, working at taking pleasure from my surroundings and my stew. Then I remembered the card. I opened it. It was an embossed invitation to the opening of a show of new paintings by a Chris Huntington.

On the back of the card, a note.

"I heard your play *A Jazz Lover* while painting in Newfoundland. I was interested in your ideas about painters. I would like to meet you."

It was signed by the artist. Well, I was sure not going to miss this. I felt quite the bohemian, sitting there, drinking rum, brokenhearted and trying to write a book. I've been trying to write a book since I was twelve. My first try was a pirate yarn that ran aground on the overwrought love story. Believe I scuttled that one around chapter five. You can't write a love story when you're twelve. I'm fifty-some now. I keep trying.

I was on the verge of happy. I poured another rum, took out my guitar and sang a song, which made me sad. She, my lost lover, was everywhere in that song. I could taste her sweet breath. So I hitched my courage up, and walked to the pay phone and called her. The pay phone hung outside the laundromat next to the hardware store. There was a streetlight that made things blue.

"Hi . . . it's me."

"Oh . . . hello."

"How are you?"

"Busy. We're editing the show."

"Well . . . reason I called . . . I got this invitation to an opening at a gallery in Halifax and I was . . ."

I could see myself in the laundromat window.

". . . wondering if you'd like to go."

"When?"

"Friday night. It's a good gallery. You should hear how I got the invitation."

"Well . . . I guess we should talk. Sure. It would be nice."

"Great. I'll pick you up at . . ."

"Why don't I just meet you there."

"Starts at eight."

"See you then."

"Happy dreams."

I walked back to the boat, stood on the dock and gazed at the schooner, gently tugging at her lines. She sat upon the breast of the bay like a gull, sleek, elegant, purposeful. *Avenger*. I'd wanted to change the name, but David Stevens, who designed and built her, didn't want me to. I listened to David. He was a Master. She is a schooner to steal your heart away. I had old well-dreamed dreams of a schooner and the deep blue sea. I wanted to share them with a woman.

It was still coolish. I climbed aboard, lowered myself through the hatch to the mahogany warmth below where I continued my journey into the rum and pondered the mysteries of love. I was beginning to think my problem was that I didn't choose women for the right reasons, that I was drawn to the wrong type. I liked them beautiful, but not conventionally so. I liked them smart and strong, but I seemed to be drawn to some kind of deep sorrow as well. There had to be something to heal, something that only my love would fix. This way goes madness.

Friday came. Before I left for town I called the woman to confirm our date. She couldn't come, she said. She was going out with the girls, but she would meet me back at her place at midnight, if I wanted. I wanted.

I went to the gallery alone. I'm uneasy at such events. I never know how to manage the canapes and the drink without looking like a goof. I didn't know anyone there and was trying to be interested in the paintings, which were solid work, nothing to lose your head over, but good solid work. I liked them. I was about to sneak away and find a dark bar when a shockingly beautiful blonde sidled up to me and asked, in a southern accent dripping honey, for a light. I swear to God, that's how it happened. Her name was Melissa.

This was the beginning of our romance. We talked til the reception was over, and then I was invited to the post opening party at the artist's girlfriend's apartment. We talked some more. But I had to be somewhere at midnight, remember? As I left, I asked Lissa for her number. She wrote it on a matchbook cover, I put it in my wallet, we hugged, I left. I arrived at My Last Duchess' place at midnight, as planned. She arrived at two-thirty.

Once, as a child on fire with the love of God, I had knelt on bare knees on a cinder path, arms outstretched as if crucified til the pain made me cry. I wanted to see the Blessed Virgin like the children of Guadeloupe had. I didn't.

2

The Fisherman's Memorial had all of the virtues of a small community hospital. I was being taken care of by neighbours who knew my story. Their concern was more real than professional. The accents I heard in the hallways were familiar and reassuring. Nowadays governments in the thrall of the corporate bottom line find such places uneconomic and the little hospital on the hill is fighting for its life. We live in difficult times.

Whatever the rules may have been regarding visitors, mine seemed to come and go as they pleased. I was almost never alone. But it's all a jumble in my memory. I'm not sure how long I was there, or who came when. I was brought food from Magnolia's Grill, a stylish little joint that Melissa had helped to create. I remember John Steele smuggling in some Irish whiskey. I remember flowers, and phone calls from everywhere. I remember staring out the window of my room at a world that looked familiar but was forever changed.

AFTER THAT FIRST NIGHT AT THE ART GALLERY, I had looked at the matchbook cover Lissa had given me. She'd written "For a good time . . . " and her number. Oh, I was charmed. I called and called. She was never there. I was very busy getting the boat ready for a summer working for the National Film Board as a "picture opportunity" in a film about the coastal parks. I was to sail to all of them to help tie the film together. The first was to be Fundy National Park, which is at the head of the Bay of Fundy, famed for having the biggest tides in the world. I was not eager to sail to a place where they remove the ocean twice a day.

So on June 14, 1980, we left Mahone Bay for Brier Island. Aboard with me was Carl Sentner, a soul mate of the rarest kind, Carl's son, and Chris Beckett, another old chum. The weather was confused. No wind, wind, rain, fog. There was a gale blowing somewhere because the sea was rough. We had problems with the engine overheating off Liverpool and so picked our way through the thick fog into Port Mouton, the nearest anchorage, and dropped the hook when we heard the surf. We were wet and tired and hadn't really got our sea legs yet.

The next morning, I rowed ashore to find a telephone and call the film guys and let them know we'd likely be a little late. I stood in the warm fisherman's kitchen like an invading alien and searched my wallet for the number. I found it, called, told them what was up. As I was slipping their number back into my wallet, I saw Lissa's matchbook cover. I looked at the number. She was on this very telephone exchange! I decided to try one last time.

"Hello."

"Melissa?"

"Yes."

"It's Tom. We met at . . . "

"It's about damn time you called!"

Oh my. This was definitely a live one. I told her I was wet and tired and hungry and needed a bath. She asked where I was. I told her. She said she'd come and get me. I rowed back to *Avenger* at high speed and told Carl and the lads they'd be keeping an anchor watch. I tried to describe the woman. They put most of it down to my natural tendency towards hyperbole.

We were sharing a rum when we heard the whistle. This was a whistle to conjure on, a piercing blast. We rushed up on deck, and there on the fisherman's wharf was a big yellow van, a big red dog and a beautiful woman. Carl and I were in the dinghy in a flash. I rowed so that Carl could get a good look at her. I remember the look in his eyes as we closed on the wharf. I believe his exact words were . . .

"Holy fuck, Tom."

"My sentiments exactly."

She shook hands with Carl, introduced us to Fynbo, the Irish setter. Carl wished us well and off we went in the big yellow van. She was wearing tight jeans, snakeskin boots, a loose fitting white shirt tied at the waist. She looked drop-dead gorgeous as she wheeled the big yellow van down the winding two lane blacktop. She was a good driver. The dog was very friendly. I was having a hard time believing any of it.

She lived in a big old one-room schoolhouse in a place called Blueberry Bay. It had tall windows and blackboards. The blackboards were full of lists and drawings and random thoughts. The drawings were bold and charming. There was a couch and an easy chair, stereo, big plank table and chairs, little kitchen off to one side, some good old dressers and such like, and a four-poster bed in the corner. The bed had been freshly made with white linens and duvet and lots of pillows. Looked like something in a magazine. Things were going rather well.

"Hungry?" she asked.

"Starved."

"I've got some fresh halibut."

"Let me cook it," I said, seizing upon the greatest aid to seduction I've ever found. Women love a man who can really cook. I can. I love cooking. She fixed me with a challenging look.

"I'll make a salad," she said. "The fish is in the fridge."

She had a good, properly seasoned iron skillet, good knives, all the right stuff. I sautéed some lemon slices in butter and olive oil, removed them when they were soft, added some garlic and pepper, turned up the heat and cooked the halibut steaks, which I'd dredged in seasoned flour. The thing about fish is get it out of the pan as soon as it's done and not one second later. Then I reduced a little white wine in the pan juice with the lemon slices. The juices and lemon went over the fish.

While I was doing this, she threw together a beautiful salad. It had flowers in it. We were getting along awfully well through all of this, as if we'd been friends for years. We sat at the table, lit a couple of candles and ate. I watched her face as she took her first bite of fish. Her eyes grew wide, she looked at me. I believe that at that moment I became something more than I was intended to be. To me, respect for food and the rituals of breaking bread speak volumes. It was the same for Melissa.

We talked at the table for a long time. I don't remember what we said. We were just telling bits of our lives, wondering where all of it might lead. Then I offered to clean up. She put on a David Allen Coe album, and blessing was heaped upon blessing.

Off the back of the big room was a smaller room with a big wood-burning cook stove and in the middle of the floor, an old claw-foot bathtub. She went to the tub and turned on the taps. As the water ran, she lit some oil lamps. I tried not to notice and took more than the usual interest in the dishes.

She was casual as she came back into the big room.

"There's lots of towels on the shelf in there. Hope you like a hot bath."

"Only kind worth having," I said as I entered the lamp-and-candle-lit back room. It was a bubble bath. I undressed quickly, hiding my disreputable underwear in a leg of my jeans and got quickly into the bath. Too quickly. It was very hot. I stood up, going from one foot to the other like a crane, felt foolish, sat down. First I took care to clean the nether regions, which caused me to bless the bubbles, since I was beginning to show my excitement.

"Not yet," I whispered to my rampant member.

As the whole world knows, the male member does not listen to the male mind, supposing the latter exists when the former is engaged. So I forged ahead, scraping off a few days of salty grime, making sure that when I emerged, I would be fragrant and squeaky clean. I was down to my toes when she walked into the room, a clinking glass in her hand. It was an Amaretto and cream. Swear to God it was. Things were going very nicely indeed. Except, my enthusiastic ablutions had dissolved most of the bubbles. As she sat on the edge of the tub and made small talk, I gathered an island of those that remained and positioned them strategically, and then took the drink so elegantly proffered. It was beyond ambrosia.

I was beginning to wonder if I was going to have to get out of the tub in front of her, thus blowing any semblance of cover, when she returned to the big room to change the record. I was out in a flash. She had great big soft fluffy towels. I dried off in a frenzy, all the while imploring Sergeant Rigid to stand easy. He was having none it. I wrapped the big towel about my middle, walked into the other room, heard Ray Charles singing a ballad, figured what the hell and shucked the towel and got in bed. The thick duvet made the sergeant's enthusiasm a little less blatant. She looked at me, I raised a knee, looked at her.

"What are you doing?" she said, all innocence, suddenly sounding like she was wearing crinolines at the cotilion.

"If I've read this wrong," I said in all seriousness, "I'm even more stunned than I thought I was."

I gave her my best shit-eating grin and she shucked her duds right there on the floor. I'll tell you the truth. Even then, after the meal and the bath and all of it and her standing there naked, I still couldn't believe this was going to happen. She was just too beautiful. Something weird had to happen. Maybe she would turn out to be a psychopath and kill me in my sleep. I was ready to risk it.

First times are usually clumsy and awkward. This wasn't.

3

FRIENDS HAVE TOLD ME THAT the accident cast a pall over the community out of proportion to what it was. We were just a couple who'd had a bad car wreck. But I'm told that people who hardly knew us were deeply affected. We were in the prayers of Tibetan Buddhists in Boulder, Colorado, for Pete's sake. I've since wondered why. Perhaps it was because Lissa and I are a part of that huge "boomer bulge" and our near deaths were a rude reminder of mortality to all in the generation who knew us. We shared one virtue. We were both emphatically alive. If we could be cut down in one random moment, then no one was safe.

On the third day after the accident I had the strength to get out of bed and hobble to the smoking room. I had five broken ribs and my right leg was dead below the knee. I could no longer imagine the absence of pain. Getting out of the bed and managing the cane and breathing was hard work. But somehow, an inch at a time, I made it. I was joined there by David, a big sweet man who'd lived a large life on the edge. A first generation Canadian of Croatian descent, he believes in the things his hands can do and his heart can feel and precious little else. We lit up, sat in silence for a while. The smoke felt ridiculously good to me. He sighed, looked at the floor . . .

"We went to see Lissa."

Where do they find that stuff they make hospital floors out of?

"Is she . . . ?"

"She's in a coma, Tom. They've got her on life support, tubes coming out of her head and every now and then she just stops breathing and lights flash and alarms go off and . . . they bring her back . . . "

David's big tears splashed on the floor.

LISSA HAD A TALENT FOR FINDING great people in those days. She was the first to meet David and Sandra. They were living in a tent, selling fruit and vegetables out of the back of a disreputable old truck in Mahone Bay. They'd just lost their farm in the Annapolis Valley to the gods that make the weather and the almighty bank. We were provisioning for our first sail to the Caribbean, our honeymoon voyage. One clear October day, the kind when you can almost see the Azores from Nova Scotia, Lissa came back to the boat laden with produce and full of joy. She handed bag after bag of potatoes and onions and turnips and cabbages down to me on deck from the wharf above. The tide was low. It's always low when you're shifting provisions. Lissa was all a'bubble.

"Wait'll you meet these folks! God, I love Nova Scotia! I told them what we were doing, that we were provisioning for a voyage, and they just gave me this stuff!"

Now she was climbing down the ladder to the boat. Her perfect ass was just perfect. A woman's bum is an endless fascination. She bubbled on.

"They're as broke as we are, for God's sake."

She arrived on deck. We hugged. A big hug full of sly intentions. Then we set to stowing the provisions and she to telling me all about David and Sandra and the kids and the truck and how the world was a great place full of great people. She was golden. She had long thick blond hair that always looked great. She had the kind of body that makes men stupid. She was happy to be what she was. She dressed to advantage, aware of the favours she'd been given and not afraid to show them in their best light. But she did all of this with such apparent ease that it was hard to catch her at it. You just came to understand that when you saw her, she would look wonderful . . . always.

I loved to watch her sleep. Her hair always looked like a movie person had arranged it perfectly on the pillow. "Ready for my close up, Mr. DeMille." If she tossed and turned, at the end of the maneuvre there it would be, all blond and beautiful and perfectly arranged on the other tack. I never figured out how she did that. Something to do with being a Southern woman, born and reared in Tennessee, the land of big and perfect hair. We were a golden couple. I'm sure we didn't know it at the time, but as I look back at the photo album, I wonder how mere mortals could tolerate us. We were having far too much fun in a world of sorrows.

Our romance bloomed in fits and starts that first summer. I was sailing to a schedule dictated by the National Film Board so much of the courtship was long distance phone calls from the VHF radio on the boat. They were often pretty funny.

"If I could just touch you . . . over."

"Where . . . over." This dripping the honey of the South.

"There . . . over." I was trying for Humphrey Bogart here. I managed Don Knotts.

The Southern Belle replied, "Oh . . . over." Her delivery was dry and moist at the same time. A considerable achievement.

I would stand at the chart table, looking out at the rugged coastline, aching for that big soft bed, listening to her voice, sometimes enthusiastic, sometimes wary. We both had good reason to doubt anything that called itself love. Our times together were short and full of passion. Our times apart were long and full of questions. We had lost at love, Lissa and I. She was more able to be honest about her reservations. I was bent on conquest, complete and unequivocal. I fear it's a guy thing. First, you win them, then you figure out what to do. If men could see the task more clearly and make sensible decisions about possible outcomes, we'd never have invented war.

My last destination that summer was Bonne Bay, Newfoundland, home of Gros Morne National Park. It was the most challenging sail, since we were getting into higher latitudes. But I had sailed hard that summer and applied every virtue I could summon to learning the art and craft of schooner sailing. We made the trip in late August, Carl and I and an unreformed hippy named Bob. He was a cheerful sort, with a tenuous grip on the planet. We were in high spirits, Carl and I. Something in the sea and the schooner and our peculiar friendship put a burnished glow on the proceedings. It didn't hurt that I was courting an extravagant beauty.

Bob was given to discussing his search for his centre. Carl and I couldn't resist. We took to calling his name softly, and pretending we weren't. Carl would be coiling a halyard, looking down, and Bob would be doing the same on the other side of the mast. Carl would whisper in a strange voice, "Oh Bob." Bob would look up, bemused, amused, bemused. Bob was a great one for musing. So in fine spirits and sweet August winds we left Mahone Bay for "The Rock," the great nation of Newfoundland.

We arrived in Rocky Harbour on August 27, 1980, at 2200 hours. It was dark. One of the Film Board guys parked on the end of the wharf and flashed his headlights to guide us in. Thank modern times for the handheld VHF. Once we were secure at the wharf, suitable festivities ensued and Bob announced that wherever his centre was, he was pretty sure it wasn't here. That left Carl and I to get the old girl home when we were finished shooting.

The end of the party found Carl sitting across from me at the galley table, the heel of a bottle of rum between us. How many nights had we howled at the moon together? We'd seen one another through some rough water over the years. Carl poured the rest of the rum carefully. We clinked our tin cups.

"So, how many minutes pass between thoughts of the Tennessee Fox?" Carl liked Melissa.

"Two, maybe three."

"And how often do you think of the other one?"

"Couple of times a day."

"Good. You're almost cured. Never liked the other one much. Don't trust fussy eaters."

"I need crew, Carl. We'll never get any sleep if it's just the two of us sailing home."

"You won't sleep at all if you're thinking what I think your thinking." Carl's big laugh filled the boat.

So there we were, salty, wild and brave. And short of crew.

I HAD TAKEN LISSA SAILING. She, like more women than men, had taken to the helm with exactly the right attitude. I had set her a task that first time.

"See that bouy?" I said, pointing to a tiny speck in the distance. She looked, carefully, systematically, and found it.

"There. I see it."

"That's where we want to go. It's a close call whether or not we can do it, and no sweat if we don't, but I'd like to leave it to starboard. If you pinch up too high, the sails will start to flap. Pull her down if that happens."

She took the helm, assuming exactly the same position that I had been steering from. David Stevens had shown me the spot. *Avenger* is perfectly balanced. Once you get her in the groove, especially working to windward, she steers herself. I watched Lissa. At first she was concerned, but she didn't turn the wheel. The boat was on course so there was no need to. This is the most profound test of the helmsman. Do you have the sense not to steer when everything is perfect? She did. After a while she let go of the helm and smiled at me.

"I believe we'll make the buoy," she drawled.

Coast Guard Radio was out of range in Rocky Harbour, but every door in the village was open and all of those within would look you in the eye with an expectant smile. I called Lissa from one of these warm kitchens. It was inhabited at the time by a mother and two sons, around ten or twelve. The boys had first appeared in my life as I stood in my underwear at the galley sink brushing my teeth the morning after we'd arrived. It was too early and the rum had taken its toll. I sensed eyes upon me. I looked up into the cockpit and there sat the lads, observing me with the interest of anthropologists. I smiled through the toothpaste.

"Like some fresh fish for breakfast, Cappy?"

I nodded. They scampered up on the wharf. By the time the coffee was made, they were back with two fine-looking haddock that they'd just caught! I was impressed. Breakfast was a rare feast.

These two excellent lads were now perched on the kitchen couch, a Newfoundland furnishing that should exist everywhere, staring at me with those curious eyes. Melissa's voice was soft on the phone. Pleasantries accomplished, I soldiered on under the boys' wide open gaze.

"What I was wondering . . . would you like to sail back from here with me? I'll get you a plane ticket to Gander and pick you up there."

"Are you sure you know what you're saying?"

Here poetry was called for, but the boys . . .

"You're a dab hand at the helm."

There was a pause here. I looked at the boys, smiled. They beamed back at me, as if in on the conspiracy.

"Hell yes!"

I could barely contain my joy. The boys were with me all the way. Mom was pleased too. I hung up the phone. There was a silly moment as all of us beamed. Mission accomplished. We had a bowl of soup.

4

THERE'S NO GOOD TIME TO BE HIT BY A BUS. Lissa and I were navigating rough waters when it happened. We were being audited by Revenue Canada and it was not going well. We'd arrived at an impasse in the relationship, and had decided to get things straightened out and go our separate ways. There wasn't a lot of anger, just sorrow that we couldn't seem to agree on what we wanted to do. I wanted to continue sailing. Lissa wanted to settle down, open another business, live a "normal life," a phrase that strikes terror in my heart. But we were resolved to stay friends. How could we not? We had shared so much, had so many big adventures.

I remember being helped on the day I busted out of the hospital and drove to Halifax to see Lissa. I don't remember who helped me. Nothing's clear to me until I found myself on Highway 103, trying to find a way to sit and drive that didn't hurt. It was a sunny day. I would flinch whenever a vehicle passed me. I had to see Lissa. There had been no good news about her, other than the fact that she was alive. I had no plan, no idea what I would do. It was just a matter of getting to Halifax and seeing her.

Highway 103 from Lunenburg to Halifax is a road I know well. It's well provided with passing lanes and you can clip right along. A couple of times that day, I tried to get up to speed, but I couldn't. Driving had always been fun to me. No more. Every time a truck loomed in the rearview, I was filled with dread. I would tell myself to settle down, but it was all too fresh. An accident I couldn't remember one second of was haunting every move I made. Somewhere in there, there must be the image of that bus.

The worst part of driving into Halifax is the Armdale Rotary. Five busy streets feed into a three-lane-wide circle. It's give and go and the devil take the hindmost and no place for dithering. As I entered it, a bus came up alongside me. My stomach rolled over, and panic almost overwhelmed me. Somehow, I held it together by talking to myself . . . "Settle down . . . you've done this a thousand times."

The parking lot at the Victoria General Hospital was a nightmare. I drove around and around, looking for a spot. I missed a couple because it hurt to turn my head and I didn't see them soon enough. I was in a bad way when I finally got one. I slammed the car into park and sat there cursing the bastard that made this sorrowful world. The pain from my broken ribs throbbed in my chest. I had to pull it together. I closed my eyes, tried to breathe softly so that the pain was easier.

"Don't think. Don't worry. Just go see her."

I got out of the car, got my cane out of the back seat, and shaped an unsteady course for ICU. The Intensive Care Unit. On the way, you pass the cluster of half-dead smokers, leaning on their intravenous drips outside the front door. Inside, a strange silence, a smell of disinfectant, a palpable sorrow. I found the directory. Radiology, Internal Medicine, Intensive Care. Second Floor.

The door is marked ICU. Behind the door, a small waiting room. A dozen chairs. A television, high on the wall in the corner. A table piled with magazines. Another door with a small window in it. Two or three people sat in the room. One look at them and I knew immediately that this was not a place you'd ever want to be. I looked through the window in the inner door. I couldn't see much. Each bed was surrounded with machines; some of the beds rocked back and forth. I couldn't find Lissa. I tried the door. It was locked. I took another look, then sat down. What was I supposed to do?

"You have to ring the bell."

"Oh . . . thanks."

There was an intercom on the wall beside the door. I pushed the button. I waited. Nothing. I pushed it again.

"Who are you here for?"

"Melissa Gallant."

Silence. Was she in there? Had she died? Would they let me in, talk to me? Finally, the door opened. A nurse with a light green cardigan over her whites led me to Melissa's bed.

"Just a few minutes," she said, and left me there alone.

The bed was surrounded by machines. Half of Melissa's head had been shaved and there were tubes coming out of it. The other half was the signature cascade of beautiful blond tresses. There were tubes in her arms and hands, and an apparatus in her mouth that I guessed was breathing for her. There was no sign of life. I stood there, leaning on my cane.

THE DAY WE LEFT ROCKY HARBOUR, Newfoundland, was sunny, the wind light from the southwest. Right on the nose. But the forecast said it would back around to the northwest by midnight and blow a small gale. We were bound south. This was just what we needed to get home in a hurry. We were well provisioned and ready to go. It was September 2, 1980. A couple of friends we'd made in the village gave us our lines and we slipped away from the dock. The crew was Carl Sentner, Melissa, and Steve Woodley and his wife, Lee Saunders. Lee and Melissa had never been offshore. I went below and got a bottle of rum and took it to the cockpit for the "rum ceremony." I took the top off the bottle and addressed the sea.

"Neptune . . . it's me again. As you can see, I have a lovely and talented crew and a fine brave schooner. Should you feel the need to test us with your might, remember, we're the ones who bought you a drink." I poured a shot into the ocean, took one myself and passed it to Melissa. She drank and the bottle made its way around the cockpit. Then I put the bottle away and made an entry in the logbook. The barometer was at 30.19 inches. The wind was light and coming from where we wanted to go. It was four o'clock in the afternoon, overcast but trying to clear. We ghosted along about twenty degrees off of our ideal course.

There was barely enough wind to put the sails to sleep. We were sailing ever so slowly in the wrong direction. I was young, awash in a high tide of testosterone and given to standing in the cockpit and shaking my fist at the heavens while shouting, "Come down here and tell me to my face why I must always sail to windward. Just because you're God doesn't mean everything you do is a good idea."

Carl was amused by these rants and he cheerfully played the Almighty's Advocate.

"I don't know, Tom. He's a busy old creator and it might not be so smart to piss him off."

"I just want an explanation. You'd figure the prime mover of the universe could occasionally come up with a friggin' explanation."

"Well, if you do get him talkin', I'd like a good reason for mosquitos. And hangovers. Friggin' hate hangovers."

By this time, I'd been sailing hard all summer long and had learned to be protective of my crew. I set the watches so that Carl and Steve and I had the darkest part of the night. The boat was steering herself so it was just a matter of keeping an eye on the compass. Coffee was made, watches were changed. I catnapped, keeping a nervous eye on the charts and making sure everyone was all right. Your first night watch at sea, even when the weather is calm, can be a little unnerving. Lee had the sunset watch and Lissa the dawn. She came on at 0600.

As Lissa stood her watch, I got the weather forecast and marked our position on the chart. We were being pushed farther to the westward than I'd have liked but the coming northerly would correct that so I wasn't too concerned. There was a gale warning, promising gusts to thirty knots. Boisterous, but manageable, especially since it would be on our stern quarter. Schooners of Tancook heritage love to run in a gale. The barometer had fallen to 30.01 since we'd set sail. Not a precipitous drop. Everything was consistent with the forecast. I made breakfast.

By 0900, the barometer had fallen to 29.9 and the wind had piped up to force five from the south southeast. This was not what was supposed to happen. We dropped the foresail and carried on. The seas were building. But it was a sunny day and the gale was supposed to back to the north so I was still not concerned. I did make a call to the Coast Guard radio station to check the forecast. They were still calling for a small northerly gale.

I sat in the cockpit and looked at things. The wind was gaining in force and it had a lot of weight in it. The seas were building awfully fast and beginning to break. At 1100 I checked the barometer. 29.0. It had dropped nine-tenths in two hours. Now I was concerned. I'd never seen the glass fall that fast in my life. We dropped the main and jib and put the helm over and lashed it, heaving *Avenger* to. She'd ride up the huge seas almost beam on and then put her bow into it. She needed more power aft or less forward.

By now the storm was furious. Carl and I went forward and reefed the jumbo, our last sail. Seas broke over us and we held on for dear life. Then she'd rise out of it and we'd tie in the reef points. As we rose out of the furious green water Carl looked at me and shouted, "No buses out here, Cappy!"

"Out where the buses don't run" had been a favourite expression of ours that summer. It described where we'd prefer to live. This was way beyond anything either of us had ever seen. But once the job was done, the schooner got her bow up more and things looked manageable. We clawed our way back to the cockpit, watched her for a few seas, adjusted and re-lashed the helm and, satisfied that we'd done all we could, went below.

It's strange how quiet a boat can be below in the midst of a furious storm. Lee and Melissa were bundled up in their berths, suffering from *mal de mer*. Steve was in the main salon, full of praise for Carl and me. He'd watched us reef the jumbo.

"That's the craziest thing I've ever seen anyone do!" he said, hugging us both. We were exhilarated. And apart from the occasional deafening crash when a sea came aboard, things were under control.

I got on the radio and informed the Coast Guard that their forecast was just a little off. Their small northerly gale had become a full on force ten storm from the southeast.

"Give me your position, over," said the Coast Guard radio operator.

"Just a minute, over." I worked at interpolating the Loran C lines, translating them into latitude and longitude. I keyed the mic.

"We're at . . . "

A fury of white noise and we were upside down. I was thrown across the cabin, mic still in hand. *Avenger* lay like that, masts in the water for what seemed like minutes, then came back up, shook herself off and carried on. The cabin was a mess. Lee and Lissa had been thrown from their berths. Carl and Steve struggled to their feet. I staggered back to the chart table, put the mic in its clip and opened the hatch. The rig was still there. She was riding it well again.

"Schooner *Avenger, Avenger, Avenger,* Stephenville Coast Guard Radio, over."

I closed the hatch.

"Stephenville, *Avenger,* over."

"Are you all right? Over."

"Took a knockdown. She seems all right now. It's pretty bad out here, over."

"*Avenger,* we have eighty knots over the ground in here. You're in a bad one, over."

"No shit, over."

"We're standing by. Check in every half hour, over."

"*Avenger* standing by on sixteen."

"Ok," I said to the crew. "That was a knockdown. I've never heard of it happening twice. Let's clean up as best we can. She's built strong. She can take it."

The words were hardly out of my mouth when it happened again. Everything was chaos. When she came back up I was about to try to reassure everyone that it could never happen again when it happened again. This time she came back with green water down below. It was up to our knees. For the first time I considered the horrible possibility that we might not make it. But not for long. We had work to do.

"Where's this water coming from?" I shouted, as Carl and I ran for the hatch. The pump was in the cockpit.

"The forward hatch is gone!" yelled Steve, who was trying to reposition the ballast forward that had flown around in the knockdowns.

"There's a rolled-up mattress forward of the sampson post. Run a line through the middle of it and shove it up into the opening. Shore it up underneath with fenders, and tie the line to the bilge stringers so it can't get away."

Steve looked at me, amazed. "Ok."

By now Carl was in the cockpit, pumping furiously. I grabbed a couple of buckets and started to bail. The sea was so furious that Carl could barely work the pump.

"Carl, come below, help me bail." It's amazing how efficient two terrified men with buckets can be. As soon as Steve had plugged the forward hatch, he joined us and we had the boat relatively dry in short order.

I checked our position. We had sea room. The wind was blowing us clear of any land.

"I'm running her off!"

Once in the cockpit, I realized the enormity of the storm. You couldn't breathe if you looked at the wind. The sea was wild with spray. The screaming of the wind through the rigging was otherworldly. I took the lashings off the wheel and waited for the right moment, then turned her. Once she had her stern to it, she took off like an escaped prisoner.

This was better. It was wild but it was better. I looked around me. Towering breakers, the sun shining through their tops, menaced us one after the other. The salt spray hurt my face like I was being sandblasted. I looked at the rig. Everything seemed secure. The tiny reefed jumbo was still there, pulling like a Mack truck. But the main was coming loose from her lashings. I let go of the helm, grabbed a jib sheet and wrestled the wet sail back between the gaff and boom and lashed it with the sheet so it would never get loose, all the while worrying that I should be steering. But when the job was done, I sat there exhausted and watched her steer herself with a free helm. She was being pulled along by the nose, keeping her stern to the fury of the seas and no sailor could have done better. I stuffed a couple of life jackets in the top of the steering box whose cover had been carried away in one of the knockdowns, and had a short word with the Creator.

"This isn't funny!"

I went below.

5

I STOOD THERE BESIDE LISSA'S BED, leaning on my cane. She was still, peaceful perhaps, but I saw no peace there. I watched her heart monitor. It was proof she was still alive. She hadn't been marked by the accident. There were no cuts or bruises. The swelling I'd heard about had receded. Except for the half head of hair that was gone and the tubes and things that she was hooked up to, she was beautiful lying there. But there was no sign of life.

I couldn't think. I was empty. Everything in our lives had changed in one instant and some kind of action was called for but I couldn't think what. I just watched her breathing, helped by the machines. If I prayed it was in a language only God could understand, but something happened as I stood there that I hesitate to talk about because it will stand no objective scrutiny except what happened in the months that followed. The despair I was feeling, the emptiness, was no small thing. I was a desert inside, arid, dry. Then, like a tropical rain, I was awash in love. Whatever needed to be done, I would do. I had the strength. I knew I did.

I carefully put my hand on one of hers, and talked to her, quietly so that no one else could hear.

"Lissa, it's me, Tom. We've had a bad car wreck and you're in a coma. Maybe that's a good idea because they tell me you have broken ribs. I do too. They hurt like hell. So you just rest there and when my ribs stop hurting, I'll tell you and you can wake up."

As I was talking to her, her heart monitor got excited.

It was going at twice the rate it was when I started talking. I took this to mean that she heard me. Medical opinion was that it was just a reflex. The doctors are wrong. I'm a doctor's son and have a deep respect for the profession. But I've observed that the more the science of medicine advances, the greater the loss in the art of it. And I am sure that the difference between a healer and an informed meddler lies in the art.

The nurse came over to me and put her hand on my shoulder. I remember this vividly. The laying on of hands. I hadn't realized that I was weeping until then. She handed me a Kleenex and waited while I got things together.

"She's a beautiful girl."

"Is she . . . will she . . . "

"You'll have to talk to the doctor. She's been very badly hurt. You'll have to think about a DNR."

"DNR?"

"Do not resuscitate. Sometimes it's better to let them go."

"Where's the doctor?"

"He's in surgery. You'll just have to catch him on his rounds."

"I don't need to talk to him about the DNR. She's not going to die. She's going to wake up and come home."

She didn't believe me but she understood me. Nurses are the great heroes of the health care system. She gently led me away from the bed and to the locked portal of ICU.

"Get some rest," she said. "Come back tomorrow afternoon. That's when he makes his rounds."

I looked back at Lissa surrounded by machines that were keeping her alive. I didn't want to leave her but I didn't want to stay there. The nurse opened the door and I found myself in the little waiting room where four sad people sat in silence. One of them, looked like the grandfather, looked up at me and we shared the little nod that is such a comfort to Maritimers. I don't think it happens anywhere else. It's an almost wink and dip of the head that says something like "Give 'er."

That's what I meant to do. Give 'er all I had. The question was how.

~

THE STORM RAGED ON. By now, it had been a couple of hours since the last knockdown. Down below, the boat was a mess. Carl, Steve and I worked at getting ballast back in place and cleaning up the worst of it. Lissa and Lee were seasick but doing their best to put a brave face on things. As he shifted ballast, Steve tried to reassure Lee.

"Everything's ok," he said.

"No it isn't!"

She was right. Everything was not ok. We were fighting for our lives. I went to the radio.

"Stephenville Coast Guard Radio, Schooner *Avenger, Avenger*, over."

"*Avenger*, Stephenville. Good to hear you, Cap. How is it out there?"

"If it can get any worse, I don't care to see it. We've taken three knockdowns. We're running off now and she seems to be taking it better, but we've lost our forward hatch. We plugged the hole, but if we go over again . . . I don't know how much more she can take, over."

"Might be time for a Mayday, over."

"What good would it do? Over."

"Any ships in the vicinity would have to come to your assistance, and we could fly out some pumps to you, over."

"All right. This is a Mayday, over."

There followed a series of questions about the number of crew, what the boat looked like, our exact position and so on. I was comforted by the operator's Newfoundland accent, the kindness in it. Then it was time to sign off.

"Are you taking water now, Cap?"

"When a big one breaks over us, some squirts in through the hatches and such, but she's holding her own, over."

"She's gustin' over a hundred in here, sir, and blowin' a steady seventy-five and you're in a bad place for seas. You'll never see worse, over."

"I sure hope not. How long do you think it will last? Over."

"Wish I could say. Probably be blown out by dawn, over."

"Ok, Stephenville. I'll stand by on sixteen."

"God speed, *Avenger*."

Every fifteen minutes or so, I'd go back on deck and watch her booming along in front of the wind and seas. It was amazing how she held her course and refused to broach. I tried steering her myself each time, and I could make no improvement so I'd return below, and go to Lissa and tell her how things were going. After a couple of hours without a knockdown, I became convinced that we would make it. It was about then that I heard the first Mayday.

"Mayday, Mayday, Mayday, all ships, all ships, come to the aid of the Schooner *Avenger*, a forty-seven-foot wooden schooner with two masts, green hull and buff deck and five souls aboard . . . "

"Hate that five souls stuff," said Carl.

"If they knew how goodlooking we are, that might help," said Lissa, which set us to laughing.

I found some oranges, cleaned the bilge water off and passed them around. The domesticity of peeling and eating them seemed to grant all of us a little respite from the horror of the storm which raged on undiminished. I spent a lot of time at the chart table, tracking our course. The one hopeful sign was that we were being blown up the Labrador Strait and there was nothing in front of us to hit. But if the wind shifted, we'd have to do something. Every half hour or so, we had to listen to the Mayday on the radio. Every half hour, we became "five souls."

"*Avenger*, *Avenger*, *Avenger*, Canadian Forces Air Rescue, over."

"This is *Avenger*, over."

"Give me your Loran coordinates, over."

I gave him the numbers. He had the same instrument aboard the airplane, so he'd be able to pinpoint the boat without fooling around with latitude and longitude.

"*Avenger*, we're directly overhead. See if you can hear us, over."

"Stand by . . . "

I opened the main hatch and looked at the sky. I couldn't see him, couldn't hear him.

"Air Rescue, *Avenger*. I can't see you or hear you, over."

"*Avenger*, we can't see you either. Too much spray. We're five hundred feet off the deck. Can't come any lower in this stuff. Shall we drop a couple pumps and a life raft? Over."

"I've got a raft. How big are the pumps? Over."

"Hundred and fifty pounds each, over."

I was crestfallen. Here was help and I couldn't make use of it.

"Air Rescue, *Avenger*. You guys know more about this than I do, but I can't see any way I could get to the pumps even if I could see them, and if one was to hit us . . . over."

"We could try and drop them up wind of you . . . but if you're not leaking bad . . . up to you, over."

"I can't see more than a hundred yards. Maybe we should take a pass, over."

"Ok, Captain. Makes sense to us. Sorry we couldn't help you, over."

"Well, thanks for trying. Is this as bad as I think it is? Over."

"Our air speed is right around a hundred knots and we're hanging up here like a helicopter, over."

"Thanks. Hate to be exaggerating when I tell this story, over."

"You won't be. God bless you, over."

"Thanks. *Avenger* standing by on sixteen."

When I hung up the mic, I stood there staring at the chart for a long time. I had four lives besides my own to consider.

How could I be sure we wouldn't need one of those pumps? I worked out our position and compared it with our last one. We were doing seven knots over the bottom, against the Labrador Current! Conditions on deck were furious. No way we'd have picked up a pump in this, supposing we could have found it. Not without turning into it and risking another knockdown. But I knew the crew was thinking, wondering if I'd done the right thing. I went on deck and steered for a half hour, trying to make things easier than they were with the helm free. I couldn't. Under bare poles I'd have had to steer, but that little reefed jumbo had enough power in it to pull her along on a steady course. I had to accept that there was nothing I could do but pump her out, go below and keep an eye on the chart. It was sunset when I left the cockpit, and it was getting cold.

Darkness fell and *Avenger* surged on through the storm. For the first time since the storm hit, I took off my foul weather suit and climbed into Lissa's berth with her. We held one another for warmth. I was shivering, and trying not to.

"Not much of a holiday cruise," I said.

"What's it like out there, Tom?"

"Majestic. Ridiculous. I've never seen such seas."

"If you had, I doubt we'd be here."

"Oh yes we would. I have to sail."

"Why do I always go for maniacs?"

Carl chuckled from the upper berth.

"It's his thing, Lissa. Everybody's got a thing."

A big sea crashed over us. Cold salt water squirted through the hatch over our heads. *Avenger* shook it off and carried on.

"Jesus, Tom, she's a fighter," said Carl.

"God bless David Stevens," I said.

Every fifteen minutes or so, I'd get out of the berth and go to the chart table and check our course and position. She was making a beeline back to Rocky Harbour. Then I'd stick my head up through the hatch and look around, using a flashlight to check the rig and the compass. The wind was holding its force, but the seas were a little less confused. There were longer spaces of relative quiet between the huge black breakers that shook her to her bones. Lissa and I lay together in the narrow berth, cold, wet and afraid. The difference was she could confess her fear. I couldn't. A crew's well being is entirely vested in the captain. If he loses it, there's nothing left for them to rely upon but a boat they don't know as well as he, and one another. David Stevens had taught me to "be calm and quiet with your crew, Tom. It gives them confidence." In all my years of passagemaking, those words have never been far from the front of my mind. If you love your vessel, which I do without reservation, you must also love your crew.

At about 0200, the radio boomed forth with a voice other than the constantly repeated recording of our Mayday. It had a plummy British accent.

"Schooner *Avenger, Avenger, Avenger*. This is the *Imperial Bedford*, over."

I leaped from the berth and went to the chart table.

"*Imperial Bedford, Avenger*, over."

"*Avenger, Imperial Bedford*. What's your position? Over."

"Stand by, *Bedford*."

I worked out our position and gave it to him.

"*Avenger*, you should be able to see us off your starboard side, over."

"Stand by . . . "

I stuck my head through the hatch and looked around. There, about a half mile off and lit up like a small town was an oil tanker. I was elated.

"*Bedford, Avenger*. You're a welcome sight."

"*Avenger*, are you ready to abandon ship?"

"Repeat please, over."

"Are you ready to abandon ship? Over."

"Sir, we've suffered three knockdowns, and had some damage, but I believe the vessel is holding together. Perhaps you could go to windward of us and offer a lee so that I could inspect things and make an informed judgement, over."

"All we are required to do is take you off your vessel. It costs us five hundred dollars an hour to stand by, over."

Carl piped up from his berth, "Tell him I've got enough for half an hour and then he can fuck right off."

"*Bedford, Avenger*. Stand by."

I went to the crew. Steven, Lee, Carl and Lissa. Dear friends and a lover. I needed to be right.

"You heard the guy. He'll take us off or carry on without us. In seas like this, taking us off involves us getting under his lee side, jumping from *Avenger* to a rope net hanging over his side and climbing up to the deck. It's very dangerous. The ship will be rolling and crashing into *Avenger* with every roll. It's easy to get hurt."

"What do you want to do?" said Lissa.

"I think we're safer with *Avenger*. The storm's still bad but I get the feeling it's losing force. We're bound for Rocky Harbour, should be there before lunch. But it's up to you guys."

Carl spoke first.

"She'd be destroyed if we tried to get off, wouldn't she?"

"Yeah, she would."

"Hell with that," said Lissa. "She's already saved our lives. We can't do anything to hurt her."

I looked at Steven and Lee. Lee was the most concerned and Steven was trying to help her through. He looked at her. She nodded.

"Let's carry on, Cappy."

Sometimes, it's very easy to love your crew.

"*Avenger, Avenger,* Stephenville Coast Guard, over."

"Stephenville, *Avenger.*"

"*Avenger,* are you ready to cancel the Mayday? *Imperial Bedford* has requested that you do, or abandon ship, over."

"I'm not all that impressed with *Imperial Bedford,* over."

"I hear you, Captain. What's your decision? Over."

"We were getting pretty tired of that 'five souls' stuff anyway. Cancel the Mayday. We're sailing for Rocky Harbour, over."

"Wind's easing some here. Should be down to an ordinary gale by dawn. Hang in there, Cap."

"*Avenger* standing by on sixteen."

6

ON MY THIRD VISIT TO ICU I finally caught up to Melissa's neurosurgeon. His name was Dr. Wholeness. I swear it's true. The kindly nurse pointed him out to me as he breezed through the room and I followed him down the hall. He went into an office and was standing there in the unlit room when I knocked on the doorjamb.

"Yes?"

"Are you Melissa Gallant's doctor?"

"Who wants to know?"

"I'm her husband."

"What do you want?"

The room was still dark. He made no attempt at eye contact and his voice was tired.

"Well, I'd sort of like a prognosis."

"She's had a catastrophic head injury. She'll never be the same. You'd better go home and get on with your life."

That was it. He picked up some files from the desk and I waited for a moment, hoping for anything. There was nothing more so I turned and started back for ICU. I managed a couple of steps, then leaned against the wall and fought back the scream that was rising. Then a hand on my shoulder.

"Come with me."

He was a young man in a white coat, curly black hair, glasses, intense. He took me to a brightly lit room. Then, as he looked through a pile of large manila envelopes on a table, he tried to heal me, like the doctor he was becoming. He was the Resident. I wish I could remember his name.

"Neurosurgeons shouldn't talk to people. They do amazing work but they shouldn't talk to people."

"No shit."

He found what he was looking for, extracted Melissa's CAT scans from an envelope, hung them on the frosted glass, flipped a switch. There, through some occult magic, was her brain sliced into sections for viewing. She was no easier to understand from this vantage point than she'd ever been.

"Look at this. See, there are hundreds of tiny clots evenly spaced throughout her brain. It's called shearing. Her brain was bashed back and forth inside her skull and everything was scrambled. There's no part that wasn't hurt. It'd be easier if there was one clot."

"So he was right?"

"We don't know that. If she was eighteen, she might make a complete recovery. The trouble is, she's forty-two. It's much harder for her. But if she's strong . . . "

"She's strong. Mean as a snake. And I know she's hearing me."

"How do you know?"

I am sure that this young resident is now a treasured healer because of how he asked this question. He was open and interested with no trace of skepticism.

"I . . . I . . . when she tries to die . . . when her breathing goes shallow and all the alarms go off . . . "

I was afraid to tell him. I was sure he'd have to say I was crazy. But he was just standing there looking at me. I took a deep breath, started again.

"When her breathing gets shallow, before the alarms can go off, I talk to her. I say, 'Lissa, you're forgetting to breathe.

Imagine a sunny day at home. You're on the Point with the cats and a good book. Everything is warm and you're lying on a quilt. Look at the cats, take a deep breath.' And she does! Two out of three times, she does. A big deep breath."

He smiled at me. And then he gave me a large dose of the only medicine that could help us in these circumstances.

"We don't know much about brain injuries. The outcomes are always surprising. We should be studying things like what you're saying but we're not. But no one can say with certainty that you're not right. Maybe her coma's not as deep as we think."

There it was. He gave me hope. I was armed for the fight. If he hadn't overheard my conversation with Dr. Wholeness, I don't know what I would have done. I would cling to his words in the storms to come.

DAWN BROKE GREY AND WAN over the storm-tossed waters between Newfoundland and Labrador. We gathered in the cockpit, my crew and I, and looked at the remnants of the storm that had tried so hard to destroy us. Nothing gives courage to the sailor like daylight. We were no longer careening through a black maelstrom that imagination could hardly bear to conjure upon. We could see the enemy, and take comfort in her diminishing powers. The wind was now gusting around thirty knots, the seas no longer breaking, though things were still lumpy enough. We mustered some grub and I got a good position and marked it on the chart.

"Rocky Harbour's a few hours that way," I said. "Let's give her the foresail."

Carl and Steve made their way up to the foredeck and I started untangling the spaghetti of sheets on the cockpit floor.

"Are you sure we need more sail?" Lee was still nervous.

"We're going to be taking the seas on the beam. We'd be going slow and rolling like a Mexican shrimp trawler without it."

"Oh."

I eased the sheet a tad, and turned her towards Rocky Harbour. She put her shoulder into it and picked up some speed.

"She's such a great boat," said Lissa.

"Better 'n I'll ever be."

"Don't be too sure."

I glanced at her. She looked great. She'd brushed her hair. I was amazed. Carl and Steve arrived back in the cockpit, cheerful. I set Steve to pumping, gave Carl the helm.

"Southeast by halfeast until I work it out."

"Aye aye, Cappy." I looked at Carl, his huge vibrant smile. We hugged. It was hugs all around and nothing new age about it. We were alive. We were bound for safe harbour. I hugged Lissa last.

"Sorry about all this."

"At least you're not a boring date."

I went below, worked at the chart for longer than I needed to. I checked the course half a dozen times. The chart was soaked and difficult to work. The parallel rules stuck and chattered. I had to get it right. We weren't in yet. At last I had a course I was sure of, gave it to Carl in degrees and he gave her a spoke or two. I got the dividers, measured the distance, estimated our speed. Three hours. In three hours we would be safe. Give or take.

"Four hours," I called to the cockpit.

"What?"

I went back up on deck. Looked for land. Something – maybe.

"We'll be there in four hours . . . give or take."

We sailed on. The ballast that had shifted up forward was all to windward so she was sailing on her bottom, giving us a gentle ride. On any other morning, conditions would have been way beyond "fresh to frightening." On this morning, we sat in the cockpit and stared at the world like it was new. Now and then a big one would stand above the rest, and all of us would watch, hearts in our throats as *Avenger* rose to it and slipped, courageous and alive, over the crest and down the other side. We were all young and on the rise and, for perhaps the first time, truly aware that we were mortal creatures and life was a precious thing.

The dark loom on the horizon became Gros Morne Head. I mentally sailed the landing a couple times. It's an L-shaped wharf in a wide shallow bay, with a long stone breakwater more or less to windward. Have to go around the windward end of the wharf and turn in bow first. How long's the wharf? How far will she carry? I'll have to get the sail off before we turn because we'll be bringing the wind aft. How many boats will be tied up? Help me, Lord.

"Ok. We'll drop the fore about six boat lengths off the wharf and the jumbo just before we make the turn. Have springs tied to both masts and ready to go. I'll take the stern line, Lissa get the bow. Make sure your coils are nice and free and get them on the wharf no matter what. Throw as if her bowsprit depended on it, which it does. We get one chance."

And so it was done. Half the town was waiting for us on the wharf. The roof under which they loaded trucks with fish had blown away. As we closed on the wharf, we could see two longliners high and dry on the beach, broken by the storm. I nodded and the fore came down. All hands stood ready. She was slowing, but there was still a lot of wind and she was moving. We dropped the jumbo. I turned, they'd made me a big empty place alongside the dock, the lines flew, and every one landed in a seaman's outstretched hands. They stopped her, we came alongside. We hung the fender boards, adjusted the lines. I went below, looked around, hugged and kissed the mainmast. I went up on deck and looked up into the faces of a village full of kindness. They were amazed that we'd survived the storm.

I climbed up the ladder thinking I'd check her lines. I turned and looked at her, listing to starboard, a mattress stuffed in the fore hatch, life jackets in the steering box. She was so beautiful. I was holding on by the thinnest of threads. A strong arm hugged me by the shoulder and led me away from the crowd, to the end of the wharf. He was an old schooner-man and he had a pint of rum in his pocket. He handed it to me.

"You could probably use a drink a dat, b'y."

As I had one drink, let it settle and had another, he pointed to Gros Morne Head.

"There's seaweed on the top of the 'ead, they were breakin' that 'igh."

I handed him the rum, he drank.

"Never want to see a storm like that again."

"Doubt you'll live dat long."

We turned and looked at the boat.

"Did she go over?"

"Three times."

"All the way?"

"Masts in the water . . . deep. Almost."

"You're back from the dead, Cap. God bless you and the man who built the boat."

"Amen."

We were walking back to the boat. Half the village was aboard, and they were stripping her. Linens, blankets, towels, clothes, mattresses, everything was coming ashore. Lissa beamed at me from the deck.

"Tom . . . these people . . . "

"There's a three-bedroom trailer up be'ind the motel. You'll stay there."

It was the woman beside me talking. Everything was under control and I wasn't doing anything. Gordon Pittman was on deck. He was the local boatbuilder and had sailed with us one day when we were sailing for the movie camera in the helicopter. That had been a week ago. Seemed like another lifetime. Gordon looked up.

"Have to make the hatch out of juniper and plywood. No mahogany in the shop. Boys'll re-position the ballast and pin it down with somethin'. Couple days anyway."

"I should check the bilge."

"Young fellas will stay with her, pump if she needs it. Get some rest, b'ys."

And so, together, all of us still unsteady on the unmoving land, we strolled up the dock towards the storm-tossed village. Suddenly we were ravenous and there before us stood the diner. Cheeseburgers! Club sandwiches! French fries! Slaw! We ate, we laughed. They had beer! They would *not* take our money. Steve, who has one of the world's great laughs, wiped the tears from his eyes and grew thoughtful. Thoughtful is another of his talents.

"Tom, when we were out there and all hell broke loose and the hatch carried away, how did you come up with the mattress solution like that? You didn't even stop to think."

I fixed him with my saltiest grin.

"Either you're a sailor or you're not," I said, and managed to keep a straight face until I had him well and truly hooked. We looked at one another, I cracked, hilarity abounded.

"Nary a bus," said Carl, and we had one of those group laughs that feeds upon itself and exhaustion finally causes it to subside among snufflings, chortles and sighs. In the calm that followed, I came clean to Steve.

"When David Stevens took me sailing that first time on the *Cathi Ann II*, he gave me the helm and went below and had a nap. When he came back on deck, he said, 'I always nap in a different berth so that I can listen to her talk. She'll tell me when she needs some attention.' So I took up the habit.

When we were sailing from Baddeck to Rocky Harbour, I went up in the forepeak and had a nap. I was lying on my back, waiting for sleep, looking at the foreward hatch. I didn't like the hatch dogs. They were flimsy. What if I lost that hatch? What could I do? I saw the mattress, the line, the fenders. I fell asleep."

"Thanks, Tom," said Steve. "I knew you weren't that smart."

"You did not."

And off we went again into sweet laughter and tears. We were hysterical.

We were alive.

7

I WAS GETTING USED TO INTENSIVE CARE. Lissa had stopped trying to die; her breathing was growing regular. When I asked how long it would be til she woke up, the answer was always "We don't know. Weeks, months, even years." I didn't believe them beyond "weeks." My ribs were healing. Friends and family were marshalling their forces and I was feeling less alone. My sister Cathy, my daughter Belinda, my mother all came to visit and stand by us. Small miracles buoyed me up when it all seemed too much.

I remember walking into the room to find Bill Stevenson, an old friend and fellow musician, standing beside Lissa's bed, gently holding one of her feet, which were turning inwards in a form of paralysis common with this kind of coma. He was singing, quietly, just above a whisper.

"When things go wrong with you, babe, you know it hurts me too."

His voice was ancient with pain and love. I stood quietly until the song was done, and then put my hand on his shoulder. Bill is not a demonstrative man. He turned, his eyes full of tears, and we embraced.

I remember my sister standing beside me, her arm around my shoulders. Cathy is strong and very beautiful. Her presence always makes me feel better. She has a powerful faith, is clear and sure of her beliefs. I too am a believer, but my way is much less sure. I can't make peace with the "One and only one way to salvation" clause that most religions contain. Cathy can, and this gives her a sureness that I often rely upon when the road starts giving way beneath my feet. We looked at Lissa, unconscious. Cathy's voice in my ear was practical, purposeful.

"Well, we'll just have to pray harder."

"Right now, every breath's a prayer."

"I know. I can see it. So can God."

"I'm glad you're so sure."

"Trust me, Tom. It's love that makes it worthwhile, and love has a name."

"I wish I was as strong as Dad."

"You are."

Cathy and I were blessed with a wonderful father. He was taken from us too early, when we were in college. But we had shared the sense to recognize his goodness when he was with us and this is part of the powerful bond we've carried through the years. I remember a day when Cathy was six and I was eight or thereabouts. We were playing cowboys and Indians with Ralph and Susan and Nancy from next door. The boys were the cowboys and the girls were the Indians. The girls made a brave charge, and we locked in mortal combat. First with guns and bows and arrows until our pretend bullets and arrows ran out, then in hand to hand combat. There was a lot of "You're dead! . . . No I'm not!" Cathy and I were flailing away at each other, hurling huge pretend punches and acting out the thing like in the Saturday cowboy movies, when I made a miscalculation and hit her for real in the stomach. It took the wind out of her and she fell to her knees, gasping for breath. In an instant a strong arm picked me up and carried me away from the fray. It was my father.

He took me to a quiet place behind the garage, put me down, sat down and collected his thoughts. I knew I was in big trouble. I stood there near tears. We didn't see Dad angry very often. Finally he spoke.

"You know what you did wrong, don't you?"

"It was an accident. I wasn't trying to hit her."

"I know that, Tommy. But you did. Most men claim they didn't mean it when they hurt a woman."

"I'm not a man."

"You're going to be. Do you know what the single most important thing about being a man is?"

"Getting a job?"

He smiled.

"No. Work is just work. The first job of a man is to protect women, because they hold the miracle of birth inside them. When you hurt a woman, you're no longer a man."

This happened a long time ago and my memory of it may be faulty. Those may not be the exact words we spoke. But the impression my father made on me that day was so vivid and his conviction was so strong that I've never forgotten the incident, the place he took me, the gentleness with which he gave me this lesson and the intent of what he said.

Cathy gave my shoulder a squeeze.

"He had the kindest eyes," I said.

"Remember how he insisted they were brown but they weren't. They were hazel."

"Hazel's not a colour, he'd say."

"He'll help us, Tom."

"He already has."

I remember standing beside Lissa's bed with my all grown up and beautiful daughter Belinda, arms around one another, all full of sorrow and tears. Belinda broke away from the embrace, used her fingers to arrange Lissa's half head of hair.

"She's gonna be pissed about her hair when she wakes up, Daddy."

"Maybe I should just let her sleep for a while."

"That would be good."

Later that night, Belinda took me to dinner. We liked pretending we were on a date, a nasty old sugar daddy and his young tart. Belinda had a sip of wine, sighed, "Well, so much for the wicked stepmother material."

The laughter was good medicine.

I remember. I remember.

We say that so easily, and have such faith that the memories are true, but they're not. They're true to who you are as you speak, or who you think you are. They're conditioned by time and point of view. They're more like paintings than photographs, full of emotion and colour and always shaped and composed by the eye of the artist. The artist is the memory, creating a background, a foundation, and a context, all of which support the individual's growing knowledge of the self and its place in this world. So who would you be if there were no memories there at all, nothing but a room full of strangers, some of them suffering, some of them moving with a purpose you cannot fathom?

Oh, I remember. The day the bus hit us I had been painting the bottom of the boat, getting her ready to launch. Lissa had been painting the interior of a house we owned on Montague Street in Lunenburg and which she was going to open as a shop. Together, we were preparing to embark on the next chapter of our lives separately, Lissa as a businesswoman, me as a sailor. We would always be friends, we resolved over and over, after each sad disagreement, after every failure of humour and compassion. From this remove, those fights seem small and foolish now. Had we known ourselves better, been less jealous of our illusive liberty, our love affair would have been much more than it was. But we were vain and secretive. We trusted too little, wanted too much and were unwilling to give without reservation. That was the style then. Sacrifice had fallen into disrepute with the rise of the hippies, who were transformed into the yuppies and so on. Nowhere in any of it had the notion that the self can only be conquered by compassion, by looking outward, even been considered. The self, it seemed, was to be controlled with drugs, first recreational and later on, when money took hold again, prescription. Lissa and I were children of the times, and even though we knew we didn't like the way things were going and sailed away from it all, our analysis was shallow and self-serving. We both wanted it all. Trouble was, we had no idea what "all" was.

ROCKY HARBOUR AND ITS KINDLY CITIZENS had the *Avenger* ready to sail again in a few days. Gordon Pittman would accept no pay for the new forward hatch and wheelbox cover.

"You're back from the dead, b'y. Your money's no good to me." And then the universal East Coast wink.

All I could do was thank them, over and over. Thank the ladies who'd done all the laundry and cleaned up the interior til it sparkled. Thank the men who'd repositioned the ballast and fixed it in place. Thank the lads who pumped her out morning and evening and kept me informed about how much she was taking. Thank the folks who owned the trailer we were sleeping in. They just smiled and winked and carried on, puzzled by why anyone would think the things they were doing for us were in any way remarkable. The mainland must be a sore trial to Newfoundlanders, with its cold indifference to the hardship of others.

I'd spent most of each day after we'd made Rocky Harbour working around the boat, or trying to. I was drawn to her each morning but found myself unfocused and aimless when I got aboard. I'd check a few lines for chafe, check the oil in the engine, and then sit and stare at her, my mind empty. Then I'd think of something I needed to do ashore and climb back up on the wharf. There I'd stand and look at her, walk away, turn back and look some more.

I welcomed any excuse for conversation about anything at all. And then halfway through, I'd grow restless and make up an excuse to be on my way. The village saw me as a brave and blessed mariner, for they knew that courage was never enough. You needed luck to survive such a storm. I had no opinion about myself. I was just there, looking ahead at the passage that remained to be sailed, or maybe I was trying not to look at it. I was moody with the crew, alternately in on the joke and completely outside of it. Alone I wanted company. In company, I wanted to be alone.

It seemed to me that the crew was dealing with things much better than I was. They talked about their feelings. They made decisions about the passage to come. They had a kind of solidarity that made me jealous. I was set apart from them and there was nothing I could do about it. She was my schooner, my dream, and I was the captain. I was responsible. I had saved them and the vessel in the storm, but I was the reason they were out there in the first place. My boyhood passions had nearly killed all of us.

One morning, four or five days after the storm, I went down to the dock and stood and stared at *Avenger*. It was time to go. Every day we delayed added to the danger that we would be caught by another gale. I climbed aboard and went to the chart table. I got the weather channel on the VHF and as I listened, I organized the charts. Once sodden, they were now dry and put away. I found the one we'd need to get us from Rocky Harbour to Great Bras d'Or and laid it out and stared at it. The storm stared back at me in a series of tiny marks made by my own hand. I was touched by the care I had taken to record the time next to each fix. They could have been written on a peaceful day but I knew the truth of it. I could hear the wind screaming in the rigging, the sea crashing down on the decks like heavy cannon fire. With great care, I found my big eraser and removed the storm from the chart, one fix at a time, so that I'd have a clean chart to work with on the passage home. Would that I could have removed the storm from my mind as easily.

That evening, over supper, I told the crew that we would set sail the following morning. This was a difficult moment for all of us. Stephen and Lee couldn't make the passage. Stephen had to get back to work, and Lee just couldn't face it again. Carl would stay as far as Baddeck in Cape Breton. We'd found another soul brave enough to make the passage in Rocky Harbour. And Lissa hung in there. She wanted to climb on a plane and fly home. I know she did. But she was never one to leave things half finished. She stayed with the boat, but she didn't do it for me. She had her own reasons. If I'd been watching more closely, and not lost in my own fears, I'd have learned something that I needed to know about her. I'd have seen her courage, her forthright willingness to face her fears and deal with them. I'd have seen the grit under all that blonde hair. But I didn't. That insight is available, even obvious, is no guarantee that it will be recognized and cherished, especially when it calls to someone who was as lost inside as I was after that storm.

It was a sunny morning. The weather forecast was benign. *Avenger* was rested and ready to go. We stowed our gear and prepared the deck. Hatches were dogged with extra care. A few of our new friends stood on the dock, ready to give us our lines. I started the engine, turned on the VHF and the Loran C. I made an entry in the log book, climbed into the cockpit, trying to present a brave smile to everyone. I looked at the village so humble, brave and kind clinging to the rocks.

"Well, time we went home. Cast off bow and stern, then give us the spring lines."

The lines came aboard exactly as asked for. I slipped her into reverse and backed her clear of the dock.

"God speed, *Avenger*."

I'm not sure who on the dock said it but it went right through all of us. We waved through tears. I turned her seaward and asked for the mainsail. We lost ourselves in the work of sailing, and soon we were slipping along under all plain sail, each of us alone with our fears. Melissa sat next to me, staring at the horizon. I looked at her profile, framed by all that wind-tossed blonde hair. We were still strangers really, held together by animal attraction and a ragged hope that time would reveal qualities worthy of love. Now we knew we could survive a storm together. We still didn't know if we could survive the day to day.

"How are you doing?"

She looked at me, then back at the sea.

"I'm scared shitless," she said. The Southern accent gave her words a piquant edge. I almost laughed. Almost.

"Take the helm while I get the weather and make a mark on the chart."

Below, I tapped the barometer, thought I noticed a tiny shift downwards, listened to the weather, thought I heard ominous signs in a completely reasonable forecast, stared at the chart and could still see the faint shadows of our course through the storm. I climbed back into the cockpit.

"Ready about."

The crew looked at me like I was crazy. We were right on course for home.

"Helm's a'lee." And I brought her through the wind. We were no more than three miles from the dock. I sailed her back there, tied her up, climbed up on the dock and walked to the end where the old man had given me the rum, and looked up at Gros Morne Head. I could see ghosts of the tremendous storm seas breaking against the ancient rock. I looked back at *Avenger*, and her brave crew waiting in the cockpit.

The old fellows who sailed coasting schooners up and down the eastern seaboard had an expression for contrary weather – "a hard chance." They would try and wait it out, but sometimes economics forced them to go, no matter how foul the conditions. This was the hardest chance I'd ever encountered and it had nothing to do with contrary weather. What I had to do was accept the fact that if I continued to sail as my old dreams wished, my destination would always be that storm. If I couldn't face that, it was time to sell the boat and buy a plane ticket. A gentle breeze was blowing that day, but it wasn't fooling me. Not for a minute.

I don't know how long I stood there. I don't remember the moment when I broke through the fear and saw the beauty of it all, the sharp plane in David Stevens' gnarly old hands as he spiled her plank, the palm and needle in Harold Stevens' hands as he worked a grommet into her mainsail, my boyish hands drawing dream schooners in the margins of my school books. We don't get to choose our obsessions. We can, if we wish, deny them because they ask too much of us, or seem too crazy. All of it comes down to having the courage to allow the heart to love what it will.

I hauled in a deep lungful of the pure salty air, medicine I grow desperate for if I spend too much time inland. "You're a sailor," I said to myself, "so sail."

I climbed back aboard, we cast her off and sailed her home.

8

MELISSA'S COMA WAS BECOMING A THING APART, an entity that people talked about like it was a place she was visiting.

"Is she still in the . . . ?"

"Yes."

I hated the word. I'd try to argue it out of existence. "She's unconscious . . . that's all. No big deal," I'd say to myself. But no amount of wishful thinking would make the coma leave the room and release Melissa back to the world.

In the ICU, you were pretty much on your own. Maybe the occasional nurse would stop by and say a kind word, but otherwise things happened without consultation, warning or explanation. One day she's on a ventilator. The next there's a tracheotomy, a hole in her throat with a plastic tube in it. "That's an improvement, isn't it?" you wonder. One day you can hold her hands, the next they're in casts. You're meant to accept this without question or comment. One day I tried to get someone to tell me what was going to happen next and nobody could. There's a lot of argument in this country about health care. Most of it ends up being about money. Money's got very little to do with the problem. The problem is that process has taken precedent over outcome. If you want a good outcome in a case like Melissa's, what you need is a caregiver willing to go the distance. That was me, for my sins. But nobody in the system noticed that I was alive. I had to get out of that hospital. I had to go home, feed the cat.

I love the drive from Lunenburg to our little house in Stonehurst, through Blue Rocks around a curve so close to the edge of the sea that when the sea rages, the waves break over the road. Tiny fish shacks cling to the rocks. Fishing boats tug at their moorings. Gulls soar overhead. Tourists stop and take pictures. They always take the same one, of a perfect little fish shack on a rock, set like an island in the cove. I took it myself that first year we bought our house. Always, the drive filled me with thanks, but now I barely noticed the ancient seascape. Now I was surprised to reach the fork in the road that takes you the last mile to the house. The last thing I remembered was walking across the parking lot at the hospital, trying to remember where I'd parked the car. How I got from Halifax to Lunenburg is a mystery.

I stopped the car in front of the house and sat there for a moment trying to collect my thoughts, but my mind felt blank. Little Bits, our favourite cat, jumped up on the hood and stared through the windshield. He looked concerned. I got out of the car and he came to me. I took him in my arms and held him close. He's a muscular grey tabby and had been a source of amusement and delight since Lissa picked him from a litter of kittens at the fish shack of one of the local fishermen. Now he was being the soul of empathy. He looked up at me. Cat lovers will know what I mean when I say sometimes you get a cat who is present, whose eyes are full of empathy and not just the empty vanity of so many of the creatures. He reached out a paw and touched my cheek. I carried him inside quickly so that the neighbours wouldn't see me weeping with an armful of cat.

Inside, I put Little Bits down and looked at the house. It was as it was the evening we left to go pick up a few folk art carvings for Lissa's shop. Ancient plank and plaster walls, whitewashed hand-hewn beams overhead. The supper dishes were still in the dish drainer. Bertha, our neighbour, had been feeding the cats and there was a collection of cans washed and stacked beside the sink. Upstairs in the bedroom, Lissa's paint-splattered work clothes were scattered about. Lissa was always good at clean, bad at tidy. My paint-splattered stuff was in the closet. I'm good at tidy, bad at clean. The book she was reading was facedown on the floor on her side of the bed. *The Human Factor* by Graham Greene. She was a smart, sensitive and constant reader. I liked that about her from the first. Everywhere I looked there was evidence of her. I picked up her overalls. They were covered with cat hair. Little Bits had been sleeping on them. He was right beside me, looking up, puzzled.

"She's hurt, buddy. We were hit by a bus."

I swear I could hear him thinking, "What's a bus?"

I'd been living out of the suitcase friends had packed for me when I was in the Lunenburg hospital. I was getting a little ripe. I undressed and went downstairs to the shower, followed closely by the cat. In the bathroom, Lissa's oils and creams. She was high maintenance in this regard. She liked the good stuff, had a passion for products from Kiehl's Pharmacy in New York long before it became fashionable. I liked that about her too. A couple of pairs of panties hung on the shower rod where she'd left them to dry. I stood there holding them, saw myself in the mirror. I remembered a phrase I'd shared with Gypsy Dave. He'd come aboard *Avenger* at four and a half with his dad, Marty Reno, and sailed with Lissa and I for a few years in the Caribbean. We grew to love him like a son. If I went ashore without him and had an ice cream cone, when I got back to the boat he'd fix me with a ferocious look. "You're in big trouble, Captain Tom."

I didn't know what to do with the panties. I looked for somewhere to put them but the problem was too big for me. I was almost frantic when I came to my senses and put them down and got in the shower. As the water coursed down over my head, I let it empty me of all thought. I just stood there, leaning against the stall.

Sometimes, you just don't know what to do.

After the shower, I put on some clean clothes and walked out to the Point. Whenever Lissa's breathing grew shallow, I would remind her of this favourite place and the hours she passed here, reading, basking in the sun. The rustic lounge chair was where she had left it. Little Bits had followed me and was looking up at me, wondering if play would be appropriate.

"Go eat a fieldmouse, buddy."

Tail erect, he began to search the underbrush.

I walked down to the water's edge. Before things had gone sour between us, Lissa and I had dreams of building a house here, over the water, with the bedroom aimed at sunrise, and the kitchen at sunset. But we'd come apart like so many do in a sad song full of selfishness and vanity, only to be fused back together by a bus, a bad corner and an instant of inattention. Had we been arguing when the bus hit us? It was possible. We were at loggerheads then, both of us disappointed and angry. We were tired, stressed out, reaching deep to find the resources to be kind, for both of us wanted to be kind. But we were a volatile mix, Lissa and I. And as I stood there, looking at our island, I couldn't shake the fear that something cruel one of us had said as we sat at that crossroads had put us in harm's way. Maybe it was me. Maybe it was Lissa. I couldn't remember.

*

WHEN WE GOT BACK TO HALIFAX AFTER THE STORM, I was numb, beyond feeling. Usually given to grand pronouncements on any noteworthy occasion, I was able only to thank the crew, Melissa included, and tell them I needed some time to be alone with the boat. So off they went, and I sat and stared at the harbour and the old wharves and wondered what to make of it all.

I had done well in the storm. I had stayed focused and endured the punishment without ever giving way to despair. I had kept the crew believing that we'd survive and we had. I had reason to be proud of myself, but that wasn't what I was feeling. I wasn't feeling much of anything, except drained and at loose ends. What was I doing with my life? Others were married and raising families, had steady jobs, volunteered in the community. I was a moderately successful practitioner of the lively arts who now lived aboard a schooner and had lost his place in the "real world."

And what of this love affair? Melissa was brave and beautiful and more than any man could wish for. She had an exotic Southern accent, a wicked sense of humour, could cook as well as I could, or better, and seemed ready to join the ship and sail away. But I was coming off a ruined love and wary, hurt and suspicious. Not so much of her, but of my ability to pick the right one. Would she turn away, as all the others had, when she learned that I was exactly what I appeared to be, and not malleable enough to be made into the worldly success that I could have been, had I cared enough to try?

Lissa was hurt when I sent the crew away. She knew she was more than crew. I saw her struggle with it, but I let it be. I shouldn't have. Why did I send her away? Love presents an awful challenge. It also presents the only true hope, but it was the challenge that I was unequal to that day. If I had asked her to stay, and she had found a way to take the burden of the storm off my heart, as she surely would, I would have been bound by love. I would have had no excuse for sorrow, other than real sorrow, nothing to ask for. Had I been brave enough at that moment, I may have found the secret. I seek it still.

I have always fallen short of what others have called "my promise." I'll have a couple of successes and then drift away from the work and become fascinated by something else, songs instead of plays, films instead of songs, a new woman, an old boat, something other than the path of least professional resistance. I've often thought that this is a flaw in my character that I should try and solve, and I have tried. I fail every time. I was afraid. Was Melissa going to end up sick and tired of my sailing through life on any wind that blew and leave me alone and broken in some distant port?

The thing I wanted most to succeed at in life was love. I have, since a small boy, cherished a vision of sharing my life with a soul mate, a woman of beauty and accomplishment, smart, strong-willed and soulful, who'd weather life's storms with me, share life's triumphs and always hold dear the love we would build between us. We'd be the kind of couple others would marvel at. We'd be seen in old age, walking hand in hand, talking like we'd just met. We'd understand one another's shortcomings and forgive them, know one another's strengths and cherish and rely upon them. Each of us would be beautiful in the other's eyes, and the changes wrought by time would only deepen our appreciation. We would be passionate lovers, intrepid friends and constant and cheerful chums.

I didn't have a lot of evidence that such relationships existed. By the time I reached manhood and was hoping to find such a mate, women's liberation had taken hold and the kind of woman that called to my heart saw all men as potential rapists at worst, and as unwitting victimizers at best. I supported women's liberation from the first, feeling that most of what they were asking for was self-evident. Equal pay for equal work. Removal of the glass ceiling in the executive suite. Sensible divorce and rape laws. I had a little trouble with abortion if it was just being used as a method of birth control but kept my mouth shut about that. But being hailed as a "good man" by the mavens of the movement in Toronto in the early seventies held no comfort. You still had to sit at the dinner table and listen to women trashing your kind with a relish that was embarrassing to behold. And entering into a relationship was stepping into a minefield that no mere man could negotiate without losing a limb. You know the limb I mean. You weren't going to bed with a woman; you were sleeping with a movement.

So it was easy to be wrong. And wrong I was as often as not. The woman I had just lost, the one before Melissa, was a complete mystery to me. She had moved to the Maritimes with me from Toronto because I had the paying gig in the family. She was an actress, often out of work. Once we got settled in, I decided that her talents were being wasted, so I wrote a half-hour film drama called *The Closet* for the CBC, and gave her the lead. I was to direct. We made the film on location in a small farming village. I'd cast a well-known Toronto leading man opposite her. We weren't two days into the filming before I could see that she was enjoying his company a little more than what was called for by the script. Right in front of me! In a film I had written as a gift for her! A film about eternal love! Jesus.

All of this drifted through my mind as I sat on the boat trying to understand. So what did I do? I climbed up on the dock, found a pay phone and called her. Halifax Harbour is an open sewer. It was low tide. The air was pungent. I dialed her number . . .

"Hello."

"Oh . . . hello."

"I'm back from Newfoundland."

"How was the sail?"

"It wasn't boring. We were caught in a force eleven storm. Knocked down three times, masts in the water. We almost lost her."

I remember a long pause here. She didn't know what to say. I sensed there was someone with her.

"I'm sorry. Am I interrupting something?"

"Well, it's just that . . . "

"Ok. I'll hang up. Nice to hear your voice."

"I'm glad you made it."

"Thanks."

I hung up the phone, empty and sad. I walked back to the boat, climbed aboard and went below. I was angry with myself. Why did I do that? What perverse impulse drew me to try one last time to repair the tattered ruins of a relationship that had provided only pain? Was it the childish vision of lifelong love, or was it an absolute inability to accept rejection? A little of both, I fear. Every failure brought me closer to the sorry understanding that my vision was a fantasy, and that there were no loves like the one I could imagine. Still, in my heart, I knew there were. I had the example of my sister and brother-in-law for one. Will and Ariel Durant for another. Abelard and Eloise. Bert and Ernie.

And there was Melissa. Now I was sure I had been wrong to send her away. If she were here, I wouldn't be alone, I wouldn't be sad, and the project of building a great love would once again be possible. But I was afraid to go looking for her because I'd been unfaithful by making the phone call. You see how crazy this is, don't you? So do I, but there's nothing I can do about it. This is what happened. This is how a man obsessed by love spends many an evening. Alone.

Avenger tugged at her lines, the dock creaked and the harbour reeked. I drank rum. A bottle of it. I sang a few songs to the empty vessel, cried a little, and talked to myself.

"You're such an asshole," I'd say. "You're weak and confused and you don't have a clue what to do."

"Absolutely," I'd reply. "Confusion is the ripe malady of the age. Who am I to rise above it?"

I was affecting a plangent Edwardian accent, staggering around the cabin in high dudgeon.

"You must reestablish contact with the Tennessee Fox, sir. You must make Melissa know that she is golden."

I took another pull on the bottle, remembered the night we met, and sat in absolute drunken amazement that I could be so wrong so often. I resolved to get in touch with her. I tried to write her a song but I was too damn tired.

With the elaborate grace of the truly drunk, I cleaned up the cabin, and went to my bunk.

9

When I got back to the hospital from Lunenburg a day later, Melissa had been moved from ICU. She was in a room with three other beds, and still, according to the nurses, deep in the coma. I didn't believe them. I took the move to mean that she was on the mend and no longer needed extraordinary measures to keep her alive. It was progress!

It was also scary. She would cough and mucus would fill her trach tube. The nurses taught me how to vacuum the thing clean with a little instrument that hung by the head of the bed. She would thrash in the bed, and pull at the restraints that tied her hands so she couldn't hurt herself. I'd try to gentle her, but she seemed at the mercy of some inner engine that she couldn't control. I felt her rising to the surface, but I was alone in this belief.

Her roommates were in bad shape too. Next to her was a teenaged girl with a head injury, who was now awake and being set upon by demons that made her scream and curse and thrash around. But every day, you could see her coming more and more into herself. I envied her family, who were now able to talk about when she was coming home, when she would be able to go back to school. They would ask about Melissa. I would smile and say she was getting better.

"That's the spirit," the father would say.

His wife would nod.

"Never give up hope, dear. It's all we have."

The thing is, it *is* all we have.

Across from Melissa, in an astounding bit of "small world" coincidence, was an acquaintance of hers from when she lived in Liverpool. We'd met her sailing in the Grenadines a couple of years before. She'd been electrocuted in a boatyard accident in Grenada, and had serious back problems. She was in constant pain, but bore it with courage and dignity. Spend a lot of time in hospitals, and you'll learn how admirable humans can be. Everywhere I looked were eyes that saw and recognized death standing at the foot of the bed, eyes that tried to hide the fear, the pain, the monumental insult that such injury visits upon you. Everywhere I looked, I saw some kind of hero mustering a wan smile.

The fourth patient in the room was a frail old lady, waiting to die. She sat in a special chair that the nurses put her in each afternoon and stared out the window, her one good hand smoothing over and over again the blanket on her lap. She was lucid but unable to speak due to a stroke. Her eyes were bright and kind, her smile was faint and lopsided, and would break the heart of a stone. She would look at me when I came to visit Lissa each day and there was in her eyes something I grew to rely upon. One day her bed was empty.

The visits were hard now. I was running out of things to say to her, having exhausted the cats, my ribs, the weather, her shop, the boat, the property. More friends could come now that she was out of ICU, but most found it difficult and came only once. It was difficult. She lay there, so still, and then she would tug at her restraints or cough, and then, just subside. Without the heart monitor to watch, there was no way to find a reaction to your presence. Her hands were in casts to prevent them from seizing up in a kind of paralysis common with head injuries, so I couldn't hold them. I would sit and pet her arm and look at her face.

It was around this time that the medical system made an attempt to communicate with me. I was informed that there was to be a "family meeting." At the appointed hour on the appointed day I found myself in a room with the head nurse, an occupational therapist, a physiotherapist and a social worker. After the introductions and some small talk, I was asked how I thought Melissa was doing. I told them that I was beginning to see signs that she was rising to the surface. The head nurse looked at me like a long-suffering teacher trying to lead a slow student through fractions.

"Melissa's coma is still very deep. We see no signs that she is going to wake anytime soon. You should visit once or twice a week and try to get on with your life. If there's any progress, we'll let you know."

I couldn't take it anymore. These people were supposed to be healers. I looked around the room at all of them, and realized that this was their job and they had another of these meetings in twenty minutes. I got up to leave, thought better of it and sat back down. I was struggling to hold my temper.

"Look. I'm a writer. Every time I sit down to write something, I have no way of knowing whether or not it will sell, but I have hope. Hope gives me the courage to do the job. My job right now is to help Melissa. I know in my heart that somehow my presence is helping, that she would have no reason to struggle back without someone calling her name every day. You people don't believe this. And you don't want to leave me any hope. You seem resolved to take from me the one thing that I need to carry on. So let's not have any more of these meetings unless you can agree that hope is the wind that fills our sails."

The social worker was a short, pretty, dark-haired girl from Labrador. Her high cheekbones and dark eyes showed Inuit blood. She had said nothing so far. Now she spoke, in a quiet voice.

"He's right, you know. If his hopes are dashed down the road, at least he has them now." She looked right at me. "I think she'll wake up. Stay by her side."

I could have hugged her.

That was the one and only "family meeting." I continued to sit by Melissa's bed and talk to her. Friends dropped in and tried to cheer me, to help me find more reasons to believe. And the social worker from Labrador who gave me permission to go on hoping will stay in my memory.

I DON'T REMEMBER WHEN I FINALLY got the courage to call her, but Lissa and I got back together and tried to forget my "I vant to be alone" foolishness at the end of the voyage. We drove to her schoolhouse in Blueberry Bay and I helped as she prepared to return to Tennessee. She planned to spend the winter there. She wasn't saying so, but I knew that she wanted to get some distance between us and think things through. I wasn't giving her much reason for optimism. I would drive back and forth between the boat in Halifax and her place, and try to figure things out. When I arrived at the boat, I would be glad to be aboard for a few hours, and then wish I was with Melissa. When I arrived at Melissa's place, I would be overjoyed to hold her in my arms, then wish I could get back to the boat.

At this remove, I think I was still in shock from the storm. People who get a diagnosis of some terminal disease often claim that once they've accepted the truth of it, every day becomes more precious. I'd been reminded of my mortality in no uncertain terms, but while it was happening, I was too busy to deal with it. The relentless demands the storm was putting on the boat gave me no time to consider the implications. I still hadn't found a way to take it all in and somehow understand my place in it. All I knew was that I didn't know.

The wonders of life were not enhanced by my new understanding of the fragility of life. Not yet.

After a couple weeks of this halting and confused courtship, it came time for Melissa to fly home to Tennessee. I drove her to the airport in Yarmouth and walked across the runway to the plane with her. There was a time when you could do that sort of thing, before the second president Bush burned so bright while being so dim. As we walked towards the plane, I told Melissa I loved her and she stopped and gave me a kiss I'll never forget. Then she walked quickly to the plane and disappeared up the steps. I stood there for a moment, then turned and walked back to the car. It's a long drive from Yarmouth to Halifax. I had time to think.

It was a clear fall day, crisp clean transparent air. You can see farther in the fall. I drove the old road, staying near the shore. I was in no hurry. If I saw a road leading towards the sea that I'd never been down, I'd take it, even though many of them were cul de sacs. I looked at lots of wharves, coves, clusters of brave and humble old houses. Then there'd be a grandiose new pile, obviously built by rich folks from "away." Most of these were empty. Why do people build houses they don't mean to live in for any amount of time?

I found myself on the wharf where Lissa had first come to get me in the big yellow van. I looked out at the cove and could almost see *Avenger* there at anchor. I imagined Lissa and I aboard, dinner in the oven. We'd be having a drink, listening to the radio, talking. Where were we bound? Far away, over the deep ocean to some magical island with palm trees and turquoise water. But what about the storms?

"The hell with the storms. You've seen the worst and survived."

I've always talked to myself. Often I say foolish things like that and try to believe them. I was trapped by my dreams. I had to keep sailing and I had to be in love. I climbed down off the wharf and walked along the beach, stooping now and then to look at a shell or a piece of beach glass. If I found something I liked I put it in my pocket, just as I did when I was a child. I was trying not to look too hard at the things I was thinking and feeling, afraid that close scrutiny would reveal how wrong I was and this intensified my interest in beachcombing. When you slip the bonds of polite society and take a road less travelled, there aren't a lot of "attaboys" available. I had a career and it had been successful while I was paying attention. Now it was slipping away.

When I was on CBC television every Friday night on *Down Home Country*, living in Toronto and making serious money, life had become too weird by far. One Saturday morning, I was shopping for groceries at the Loblaws nearest my apartment. I was probably hungover. As I stood staring at a shelf of cereal, trying to decide which one to buy, a woman of a certain age walked up to me.

"Are you Tom Gallant?"

"Yes."

"You look much nicer on television."

What was I supposed to say to that? I had a team of experts, hair dressers, makeup and wardrobe people who were paid well to make me look great when I was on television. This was Saturday morning, and I'd pulled on some jeans and a t-shirt and staggered down to the store for groceries. I was about to apologize for looking so bad when she just walked away. I grabbed some meusli and made for the checkout counter, head down in the hopes no one else would recognize me. The checkout girl was all smiles and eyelashes. I guess she approved of the rugged, unshaved me. I paid her, took my groceries and got out of there.

The walk home was a nightmare of sidelong glances and knowing smiles. I loved it when the old urban blank look was all I got. I was not taking well to fame. I felt like my fly was open or that I had a piece of spinach caught between my teeth. I wanted my obscurity back. For twelve years I had fought my way up in show business, only to find when I arrived that the price was too great. So I moved back to the Maritimes and bought a schooner. Now I walked a beach alone, wondering if I'd done the right thing, ever. I was ashamed of my confusion, well aware that there are people in this world to whom time to muse about such trivia would be sweet release from the urgent need to find food, safety, a dry place to sleep.

As a child, I had liked digging wells in the sand and watching them fill with water. I found a big clam shell and dug a nice deep one, about a foot in diameter, and sat there and watched it fill. You dig in the hard sand just below the high tide line and the hole fills quickly. Then I dropped my beachcombing treasures into the water and watched as the sides of the well eroded and fell into the water. The afternoon breeze was up, riffling the cove with whitecaps. It was a nice day for a sail.

I walked back down the beach to the car. Nothing had been solved. But a well had been dug and a treasure buried.

10

I WALKED INTO THE WARD mustering what little hope I had left, saw Melissa lying there unconscious and cursed the fates that brought me to this pass. Were the doctors right? Why shouldn't I just turn and walk away? What had I been thinking when I made all those vain promises to her, to myself? I stood there at the foot of her bed and couldn't think of a thing to say or do. She didn't know I was there. I looked at her and felt empty and tired. The room was ugly. Why must hospital rooms be ugly? She was oblivious. Her roommates were healing or dying. She was oblivious. I turned and walked away.

On the elevator, I let myself think about the evening ahead. I'd go to a bar and find someone to talk to who knew nothing about me or my troubles. We'd talk about the weather, baseball, sailing, late Victorian architecture, anything but comas. I'd tried. For over a month, I'd spent every day by her side. I'd refused to accept the verdict of the experts. I'd talked to her, prayed for her, wept bitter tears. I needed a rest. My ribs still bothered me. My leg was still numb.

The elevator doors opened. I walked through the lobby and out into the daylight. I took out a cigarette and stood there flicking my Bic. The thing was dead. Little frustrations like this can send the tired soul over the edge. I looked at the blue summer sky and took a couple deep breaths. Off to one side stood the usual cluster of smokers, leaning on their IV's, puffing resolutely. I got a grip on myself, joined them and asked for a light from an impossibly thin fellow in a funny housecoat that looked like it belonged to his wife. He had a Zippo with a navy crest on it and he liked using it. It clicked shut with a satisfying mechanical authority.

"Thanks."

"No problem. Nice kind of a day."

"So far. What're you in for?"

"Cancer. Lungs are full of it."

I wanted to laugh. He took a long drag, exhaled. Smiled at me.

"Started smokin' when I was nine. Players Plain. Always knew they'd catch up with me. Tried quitting a couple of hundred times. Couldn't. Trouble is, I love the damn things. Too friggin' late now."

"You getting chemo?"

"Nah. I'm just dyin'. What the hell. Had a good enough run at it."

"I know how you feel." I really liked this guy in his funny housecoat.

"You're too young to know anything about dyin'. I was your age, I thought I'd live forever."

"Yeah . . . well, you get reminders that it won't last forever."

"Heh. Like maybe, W.W. Two. I got torpedoed twice. Never wised me up any. What're you doin' here?"

"Wife's in a coma. Car accident."

"Shit. You're in more trouble than I am."

"You're dying, for God's sake."

"Yeah, but I won't have to watch my wife die. I couldn't stand that. Like I said, I had a good run at it and I won't miss nothin' but her. When it's over, she'll just carry on, givin' the grandkids more time than she can now. She'll be ok. But if she went first, I'd be no good to anyone. She's stronger than me."

"Lissa's not dying."

"That's the spirit. Just like me floatin' in an oil slick in the North Atlantic. No way I was gonna die." He choked out his Players between his finger and thumb, rolled the tobacco out and made a tiny ball of the paper and flicked it away.

"Called that 'field dressing' in the war. I guess they didn't want the enemy smokin' our butts. Never made sense at sea, but I been doin' it since basic training. Wouldn't work with filters."

"Don't suppose it would."

"Well . . . back to the salt mines . . . " and he took hold of his intravenous contraption and shuffled off. I finished my smoke, pinched off the ember, rolled out the tobacco and put the filter in my back pocket. Then I went back into the hospital and pushed the button for the second floor. Figured I'd tell Lissa about the guy with the Zippo and the Players unfiltered cigarettes. She always liked guys like that.

WINTER LOOMED LIKE AN ELECTION and I needed a place to put the boat where I could live aboard. Living aboard a boat in the winter in Nova Scotia may be foolhardy, but you wouldn't think it would be such a trial to find a place to tie up. The yacht clubs will let you wet store your boat but they won't allow you to live aboard, and most government wharves will send you away, so you have to find a private wharf in a well protected place because the winter gales can be fierce.

So I sniffed around the waterfront and endured all manner of scepticism and dismay from those I asked for safe harbour. Canadians are a worrisome lot, and there was more talk of insurance than I find wholesome. Insurance is a scourge on the independent soul. The very idea that you can buy protection from future calamity strikes me as foolish. Think about the rise of the idea of "life insurance" long enough and you're soon a dog chasing his tail. Boat insurance is particularly strange. The farther you go offshore, the more it costs, though any deep water sailor will tell you that it's where the water meets the rocks that danger lurks and the more you sail deep water, the more committed you are to living a long and lovely life.

Danger. Society has a pathological fear of danger that seems to grow and mutate with every passing day. As a child, I rode my bicycle without a helmet, climbed trees and rock faces precipitous enough that I well and truly feared for my life, with no more than the occasional reminder to stay out of the traffic. There were skinned knees and elbows but no broken bones. Now, there are laws that try to make childhood perfectly safe. The old and disappointing myth of security passes from religion to commerce and some things get better and some things get worse. But are the kids better off for all this official concern? They seem a timid lot. All the safety courses and dire warnings seem to be producing a generation of blumpy couch potatoes, expert only in video games. Bring on the punks in chains. They give you hope.

I remember venturing off on winter camping trips with a couple of buddies when I was around twelve. We'd leave on Saturday morning and return Sunday afternoon. Our packs full of cans of beans, bacon, eggs, and tea, some carefully packaged packs of wooden matches, we'd don our snowshoes and head "back the woods." We knew the trails fairly well, and had the sense to mark our way with hatchet blazes on the trees if we decided to try a different way. But this was northern New Brunswick and the snow was deep. I doubt modern parents would allow such adventuring. Oh, it was glorious.

We'd take turns in the lead, cutting the trail, and try to move silently, watching for signs of animal tracks. From morning to late afternoon, we'd press on, just stopping to eat the sandwiches we'd made for lunch. When we found a good place to camp, we'd go to work. First we'd beat the snow down with our snowshoes in a manic pagan dance, making our floor. Then one of us would gather wood for a fire, while the other two built a lean-to for shelter. We had hatchets and we'd cut a couple of small trees for the frame, and use the boughs for the roof and floor. Usually, we'd pick a place where we could dig into a snowbank with our folding war surplus shovels. We were very proud of our skills as woodsmen, and talked about how it must have been for the pioneers who first opened the land. We'd find a fallen tree, wet and full of rot, and split it and make a foundation for the fire. This kept it from sinking into the snow. Once the fire was built and the kettle full of melting snow for tea, we'd explore the terrain around the camp. There's a silence in the winter woods, and the air is clean and crisp. There are no bugs. Only the occasional owl, or rabbit. Sometimes, a deer. We were the only people in the world.

We were free. We were on our own. I know our parents worried from the time we left til we returned, but they allowed us to go and they did it because they thought it was important for us to challenge ourselves. We took pride in building a fire that would light with one match. We made sweet strong tea and cooked our supper, usually fried baloney and beans and a fire roasted potato each and no food ever tasted better. Then we'd sit in the shelter, and keep the fire burning long into the night as we shared stories and dreams. I don't remember what we said. But I perfectly remember what it was like to be there.

When the talk was exhausted, we'd climb into our sleeping bags, fully dressed but for our boots, which we'd stash in a dry place, and our parkas, which we'd roll up for pillows, and the talk would grow sporadic til sleep finally came. I would lie awake, and invigorated by an atavistic fear of the dark silent woods, think about what life was, what I would be. I had all kinds of notions – some like those we spun out around the fire – from fireman to pirate to hockey player to jet pilot but I always came back to my secret vice. I could talk about it with Dicky and Burnsie. I wanted to be a writer, which I was pretty sure involved smoking cigarettes and drinking hard liquor and living in a dangerous foreign city. Where I got this information, I don't know. I was a precocious reader and mostly unsullied by television. I thought it was cool to write poetry or novels, to be an actor or an artist, but I kept that affliction under wraps, except for winter camping trips with good chums. Northern New Brunswick was a hard and beautiful place and impatient with anything that looked like pretension.

But what about East Tennessee? Did Lissa go camping? Was it anything like what I lived? She'd told me a lot about growing up. Her Momma, born in a hollow in Bristol near where the Carter Family of country music fame was from, wanted to move to town and have the finer things. Her Daddy (Momma and Daddy are Melissa's words) hadn't finished high school, but he had been a canny and successful businessman, buying low, selling high and always moving forward. He had provided a low-slung brick ranch style house on the fairway of a golf course in Kingsport for his family while still clinging to his love for the hillbilly "a man's word is his bond" way of doing things. He collected Civil War flintlock rifles and had a peerless eye for fine handmade things. He bought a lot of land with a sage sense of what would happen to the town. His nickname was "Greaser (pronounced greezer) Groseclose" because he was good at grabbing and holding on to the greased pig at the county fair. I swear it's true. Melissa told me. I've seen a wonderful picture of him, shirtless, shoulders up and arms aflap hot on the heels of an agitated pig in full flight. He was short and stocky and had thick curly black hair.

This is all about memory. I know it's getting out of order, but that's the way memory is.

By now I had read all the available writing, and there's not much of it, about brain injuries. I knew her memory was going to be hurt. I didn't know how complete the devastation would be. The experts had painted such a dark picture. I thought about it constantly.

"When she wakes up . . . what if she doesn't remember him? What can I give her of her Daddy?"

I wasn't really there. I never met him. She'd be rebuilding her life based on hearsay. At least she was the source and I had listened hard. But what did it feel like to be twelve in Kingsport, Tennessee? How did a flashing blonde Southern beauty of the kind who could have had anything in the material world by merely smiling and saying "yes" end up living alone in a one-room schoolhouse in Blueberry Bay, Nova Scotia? I knew some of it through the empathy we shared. Our outlaw selves were always in accord. I knew I could tell her that she loved and admired her Daddy, while seeing clearly the limitations of his world view, which was encompassed by a life lived entirely in East Tennessee and surroundings. He knew what he knew very well, but what he didn't know was a mysterious and alluring place to his little girl, golden and pretty, her eye on the far horizon. But he had loved her well and kept her in hot cars when she got her driver's license. I remember vivid stories of a Triumph Spitfire and a Chevy Malibu Super Sport. I like that he gave her those cars. He loved her wild streak. He wasn't afraid of it, nourished it instead of putting it down.

I could tell her that her mother was a "lady" and that they had conspired to buy her new dresses without her Daddy knowing. I could tell her that her Momma loved her but they argued when she went through her hippy phase and stopped shaving her legs. And I could tell her that her Momma was a fine woman with a true heart and a sense of humour and the rightness of things.

And I could tell her that both her Momma and Daddy were dead.

I FOUND A BERTH THAT WINTER IN MELVILLE COVE, in the Northwest Arm of Halifax Harbour at a floating raft in front of James Rosborough's place. He was a designer of little ships that looked like something from the seventeenth century. As the weather grew colder the cove iced over, and I would use my boathook to break it up as I struggled ashore in the morning. When the ice got thick enough, I'd be able to walk to the boat, but the transition period was getting to be quite a trial. Then, one morning as I pulled the dinghy up on the floating dock by the shore so it wouldn't get frozen in, I was met by a stranger with a round, smiling face and a thick Czech accent.

"You can't do this. You have to wait for the ice to get thicker."

"Maybe I can keep one path open til the rest is thick enough to hold me."

"You'll freeze to death. My house is right there. I have a spare room."

And that is how I met Paul and Ethel Toman, two of the kindest people in the world. I moved into their spare room, and we shared a wonderful winter, cooking together, laughing and becoming friends. When the ice was thick enough, I would visit the boat each day, chip the ice out of the bilges, build a fire in the coal stove and dry her out inside.

Once the fire was built and the boat warm enough, I would sit at the table and read Lissa's letters from Tennessee. I would write her long rambling answers to the questions she asked, trying to set her heart at rest, and mine. I thought I was telling her the truth. I wonder now sometimes if I even knew what it was.

11

EVERY DAY I WENT TO THE HOSPITAL, and every day it was the same. By the sixth week, I was numb to everything but the ferocious hope that she would wake, and we would make a miracle. One evening our friends Arthur and Susan were visiting. As always, there was much talk about any signs that she was surfacing. After exhausting my optimism I left them with her and went down for a smoke. When I returned, the two of them were all smiles. She had opened one eye! I went to her, called her name. She turned her head slowly and that one eye looked at me. I couldn't believe it.

"Give me a kiss."

Her lips pursed slightly. I kissed her, and felt her kiss me back. It was, and remains to this day, the most perfect kiss. It contained no wish for satisfaction, no quest for more. It was just what it was. A simple, heartfelt kiss of friendship, of recognition, of love. I fell to my knees by the bed and wept. Our strange voyage towards the light had finally begun.

Melissa and I were rich in friends and during this time they were attentive and giving beyond what anyone could expect. Now that she was awake they came in droves to stand there and look into her one open eye and share her crooked smile, all of them bearing their gifts of hope and humour. I wonder if we'd have made it through without them. I doubt it.

THE ICE LEFT MELVILLE COVE EARLY, and I moved back aboard the boat, though it was difficult to leave the home that Paul and Ethel's had become. Getting *Avenger* ready for another season of sailing was the finest kind of work. Bending on sails, recomissioning the engine, organizing the forepeak, oiling the blocks, checking lines for chafe. Owning and sailing a traditional schooner is a process of constant learning. Many of the skills involved are ancient and almost lost. You make your own tools, seek out the old masters. The more the vessel asks of you, the more you do for her. The more you do, the deeper your affection. Just as it is with people.

Lissa returned to Nova Scotia with the geese, opened her little house in Blueberry Bay and we began our courtship anew. She came to Halifax and threw a huge birthday party for me at Paul and Ethel's place. She made a big pot of Texas chili and a sinful cheesecake and the guest list showed me that she'd done her research well. All of my closest friends were there, and she had endeared herself to every one of them.

What I remember of that summer, 1981, is the way we moved back and forth between her world and mine. I sailed to Port Medway to be close to her. She sailed from there to Chester with me to do the schooner races. Her confidence and affection for the boat grew as we sailed together. She had an instinctive eye for the sails. She could tell when they weren't right even before she understood why. She moved around the boat gracefully and soon did things before I needed to ask. During the races, she worked the foredeck wearing a bikini and a rigging knife in her belt. This gave me a great advantage at the starts, since the rest of the fleet was staring at her

extravagant beauty and not paying attention. It was a tactic I employed for years, each year adding another of Lissa's gorgeous friends, til the rest of the skippers were begging for mercy.

There were many of the precious diamond days that Nova Scotia provides in the summertime. The climate here is often harsh, so when it does get warm and easy, it has a kind of glory and wonder, the more so because you know in your heart it can't last. Nowhere else I've been is as radiant. We would anchor in some deserted cove and row ashore and walk the beach. Then we'd row back to the boat at sunset and cook a meal together. Sometimes there were friends with us. Sometimes we were alone. It was starting to look to me like we could make a good life together.

Professionally, I was drifting away from television and back towards live theatre, my first and deepest love. It didn't pay as well, but in every other way the satisfactions were much greater. John Neville, the great English actor/director, was the Artistic Director of Neptune Theatre in Halifax and was opening the coming season with a play of mine called *Step/Dance*. And he had asked me to be the theatre's Artist in Residence. So we had a little money in the kitty and the promise of a winter full of satisfying work. It was easy for Lissa to imagine that I'd be a reliable provider, which was important to her. That she was a tad overconfident in this regard was not something I was eager to tell her. The freelancer's life is one of feast or famine. She'd learn that soon enough.

So we sailed together, and revelled in the sweet summer breezes. Nothing remarkable happened. There were no storms, no tragedies, nothing for us to do but grow closer to one another. Were we mindful of the blessings at hand? Not as much as we should have been, I'm sure. Both of us had a small gift for noticing that we were having a good time, but I now know that we didn't let the pleasure go deep enough. If we'd had a clear vision of the pain to come, the sunsets would have been even richer.

As August drew to a close and the evenings grew chilly, we sailed to Halifax and found a berth for the winter at the Maritime Museum of the Atlantic. I winterized the boat, building a wood and canvas "back porch" over the cockpit and house, and began work at the theatre. Lissa made a trip to Tennessee and while she was gone, I had a double berth and some bookshelves built, a surprise for her when she returned. We had shore power, a phone and I installed the little cast iron coal stove in the galley.

We were very happy together that fall. The play was a success, and life aboard the *Avenger* was a rich adventure. We listened to CBC Radio, read good books, cooked wonderful meals, and made love as only new lovers can. I remember one night when an easterly gale blew up, and we were getting pounded against the dock. We got up and the two of us rigged breast lines to the windward dock, no easy task at the best of times. There was driving sleet and the wind was bitter cold. I took the lines to the other dock and made them fast and returned to *Avenger*, slipping and sliding on the sleet-covered surface. Once I was down on the deck, we worked together, waiting for the lulls, hauling her off the dock til she couldn't hurt herself anymore. Then we went below and built up the fire in the coal stove.

"That was different," said Lissa as she made us hot rum toddies.

"You were great," I said. "You understood how to work with the sea. When we had the advantage, you used it well and never lost an inch of line."

"This isn't how I pictured yachting."

"Me neither. I've always had visions of tropical islands, palm trees, turquoise water."

"Next year," she said as she handed me my drink.

My big dream was coming true. I would sail away, and I would not be alone. Melissa would be beside me. It was around this time that we started talking about getting married. Lissa was more than wary about it. Of course I took this personally. But I tried very hard to understand her fears, to see them from her point of view. If I could have taken myself out of the equation entirely, I'd have found the insights I needed to recognize her real needs and my capacity to provide for them, or not. But I was bent on conquest, and therefore a fool in full.

The Christmas production at Neptune that winter was *Guys and Dolls*, surely one of the best Broadway musicals of all time. I'd had great fun playing Benny Southstreet. Right after Christmas, which we'd had aboard the boat, Lissa flew to Tennessee to be with her mother, whose name was full of

Tennessee charm. Thelma. I drove down with the announced intention of asking Thelma for Lissa's hand. It's a long, long drive but I made it in thirty-six hours. Lissa met me in a waffle joint where I'd found a pay phone, and led me to her home. Thelma met us at the door. She was perfectly put together. Her wig looked regal. She wore it because her head was full of cancer and bald from the chemo. She was beautiful.

Lissa went to bed early that night, leaving Thelma and I to sit up and talk. The first thing I asked her when we were alone was how she was feeling.

"Ah'm pretty much settled with what's happening to me, but Ah do worry about Joey and Lissa."

"I don't know Joey so I can't say how he'll do, but you needn't worry about Lissa. She's a strong one."

"She always was the one venturing off. Couldn't let her out of mah sight when she was little."

"That's why I love her. I came here to ask you for her hand."

"Well, that's a pretty thought, but what Ah say isn't what's gonna matter with her. You're gonna have to talk her into it."

She was sitting in a platform rocker, composed, rocking back and forth gently. There was the ghost of a smile.

"Suppose I can manage that, would it be all right with you?"

"Well . . . there's not a lot of men would drive all this way just to talk to me and that's in your favour. Ah just hope you'll be a good provider. Ah'm afraid Ah gave her an appetite for the finer things."

"I've noticed. I've made some money in my time."

"You just keep on doin' that."

"I'll try."

We sat quietly for a while. Lissa and I had talked a lot about the cancer. My father had died from it, and I knew what it was like to have to watch the slow slipping away. Then, hurt as I was at the thought of losing him, my sympathies were with him, for he was losing everything. Now I looked at Thelma, rocking, looking at her hands folded in her lap.

"It's a lot to say goodbye to, isn't it?"

She looked up, then down.

"It sure is. But Ah'm not so sad about it for me. You grow up practical on a farm. It's just part of life. Ah know Lissa and Joey are grown up, but they'll always be babies to me, so Ah worry. Ah know it's foolish."

"It's not foolish. I've always been impatient with worry. I see it as robbing today of its joy because of something that might or might not happen tomorrow. But in this case, you know what's going to happen, and . . . "

"Ah don't want them to take it too hard."

I was very moved by her courage and compassion.

"When my father died, I thought I'd never get over it. And I never did in a way, but the grief became different over time. Now it's like an old friend. It reminds me that love can go that deep."

"That's just how it is. You've got a way with words, Ah'll say that for you."

"It's my job, Thelma."

"Well, maybe you will be able to make enough money to take care of Lissa after all."

We laughed together, the laughter of recognition. Then she went to bed, and I sat there for a while, in a house still strange to me, trying to imagine what it was like when Lissa was young and the family intact.

12

It took a few days to convince the professionals that Lissa was awake, even though that one eye opened every day for at least an hour or two, and when it did and looked at me, there was that small, crooked smile. But finally, all agreed that the coma was over and the tracheotomy was closed and she was breathing on her own. She began to eat a little solid food, though she was as messy as a baby when you fed her. She was a baby, though I was sure that somewhere in there the woman I knew must be hiding.

The first sign of progress was the return of her prodigious appetite. Soon feeding her was like feeding a baby bird. You couldn't get the food to her mouth fast enough. She was ravenous, having existed on nothing but liquids through an IV for the six weeks of the coma. As fast as I'd shovel it in, she'd swallow it down and be waiting impatiently, mouth open, an urgent look in her eye before I could reload the spoon.

And then another sign of healing. She began to make faces when the same grey mush turned up at every meal. I knew how to fix that. I went to a fruit stand and bought a couple of ripe mangoes. In our years sailing the tropics, we'd both developed a powerful affection for tropical fruit. I don't think she knew what it was while she watched me cut it. At least, there didn't seem to be any sign of recognition. But when I put the first golden morsel in her mouth, that eye opened wide, the crooked smile grew til juice ran down her chin. And then, a single tear ran down her cheek.

"Remember, Lissa?" I said as I delivered sweet bites of mango to her open mouth as fast as her urgent desire dictated. "We sailed *Avenger* to the islands. We used to have mangoes and papayas for breakfast almost every day. You used to dive over the side every morning and swim a few laps around the boat. Your favourite islands were Anguilla and Bequia. Remember?"

As she dispatched both mangoes, her face awash in the sweet juice, I prattled on about the islands and what we did there, the people we knew. I couldn't tell if she was getting any of it, but she listened intently. When a silence came, and I was wiping her face with a damp cloth, I thought I heard her say something.

"What?"

"Good."

Her voice was hoarse, low and faint. But I heard her.

"The mango?"

"Good."

"I'll bring some every day."

When I finished cleaning her up, her eye closed and she went to sleep. She looked like her old self when she slept if you found a perspective that hid the side of her head that had been shaved and was now growing stubble. I straightened the luxuriant blond tresses that were still there like she used to do in her sleep. I sat and stared at her for a while. It was heartbreaking some days, heartening others.

THE HALIFAX WATERFRONT STILL HAD some of its old ramshackle crankiness in those days, though it was obvious that the whole thing would soon be gentrified beyond recognition. When spring came and we began to get the boat ready for the sailing season, Lissa found an ad in the paper that filled her with inspiration. The Government of Nova Scotia was calling for proposals for touring shows to help celebrate "Come Home Summer," a tourism promotion that was designed to bring the Nova Scotians who'd left home to make a living back for the summer. It actually worked.

Lissa's idea was that I would write a show that we could tour under sail. So I wrote the proposal, it was approved, and we were being paid to go sailing! Neptune Theatre would be dark for the summer, so the timing was perfect. *White Sails and Tall Tales* was a gentle little show, a concert of sailing songs and sketches that we took to almost every little port in the province. It was our first venture together, and in it were the seeds of our goodness together, and the weakness that would pull us apart.

We were full of fun and optimism that spring. As the winter cover came off the boat and light poured into the cabin for the first time in months, we made lists and love and watched in wonder as the plans we made fell into place as if by magic. We knew we would need a bo'sun for the summer, a hardy sailor who could tend the vessel when we were doing the show. Enter François Tanguay, an ex-fisherman from northern Quebec on fire to go to sea. He was rough around the edges, strong as a bull, uncomfortable speaking English and utterly reliable. Lissa and I liked him instantly, and when we both liked someone, we were usually right. We pointed out his berth, he came aboard, the boat started coming together and he and Lissa began a cribbage tournament that was to last the whole summer.

We needed a cast for the show. We'd both agreed that Bill Stevenson, a great jazz piano player and singer, and his wife Betty Belmore, a rare and wonderful singer with a special gift

for harmony, would fit in perfectly. They were friends, they loved to sail and they were very good. Then there was Chris Beckett, who had a big burdensome ketch called *Rorqual* and could play guitar, fiddle and mandolin and sing. All we needed to round things out was a lead guitar player who could sing and act.

One afternoon, as we sat in the cockpit sharing a tot of rum, a man with a guitar, a cowboy hat and boots and a small boy in tow ambled down the dock. It was Marty Reno, an old friend and one of the best singers, songwriters, guitar players in the country and the boy was Gypsy Dave. Marty's family had come apart, and they were at loose ends, looking for something to do. Marty got the lower berth and we made a hammock over that for Davey. We eighty-sixed the cowboy boots and hat and got him some deck shoes out of production money.

Rehearsals were held in one of Neptune's old rehearsal halls and the show came together quickly. There was a sense of adventure in all of it and as we booked the ports we would sail to, Lissa found and bought the clothes we would wear on stage and off, had t-shirts designed and made for sale before and after the shows, and set up the books. She was proving to be a great partner, a first mate for sure.

We were eager to get out of Halifax Harbour, which grows ever more pungent as the weather warms. So we booked a haul out at the Oak Island Marina and set sail for Mahone Bay. It's a day sail when the wind's right, and the crew was Lissa and I and Marty and Davey. This was Marty and Davey's maiden sail. We were late getting away from the dock, and by the time we were off East Ironbound Island, things were gnarly. The wind was blowing hard, the fog was thick and the night air was cold. This was before the Global Positioning System was in place and navigation was the ancient art of steering a good compass course, knowing the tides and how fast the boat was moving. As we slipped under Ironbound, moving fast enough to leave no margin for error, I was very eager to find the buoy between it and Tancook Island, to see it clearly enough to read the identifying letters and numbers on it. Lissa was on the bow, listening for the bell. I was at the helm. Davey sat below, his chin on his arms on the table. Marty was with me in the cockpit.

"Get me the flashlight, Marty. I want to read the buoy."

Marty flew down the companionway ladder and commenced to search for the flashlight. Davey saved the day.

"Dad . . . it's right there."

As Marty handed me the light, Lissa called from the foredeck.

"It's off to starboard, I can hear it."

"Don't let me hit it, but get me close."

Lissa pointed at the sound, and then . . .

"There . . . I see the light."

A faint green light flashed in the fog. I steered for it, and as we went by, I read the thing and confirmed our position.

"Come steer, Lissa. I'll get your course. Marty, you keep a lookout, and let me know when you hear the surf."

Marty was sure we were going to die, but loving the whole thing anyway. With Lissa at the helm, I laid a course that would take us between Big and Little Tancook, and gave it to her. Marty let us know when he heard the surf. We conned her through the cut and anchored in Northwest Cove off Big Tancook. We still couldn't see the island.

I praised Davey for finding the flashlight so quickly, Lissa poured some Jack Daniels, and we settled in for the night. We four would become a family in the years to come, sharing adventures and heartaches, learning the mysteries of the deep ocean together. Time and circumstance put us together, love and good humour kept us that way. Of all of Lissa's virtues, and they were many, her ready acceptance of the sweet souls *Avenger* drew to us over the years was the greatest. She would give freely of her love and concern and make everyone feel at home aboard the boat. She had a genius for empathy.

When morning came, and the sun burned off the grey, we gloried in the beauty of our surroundings, made a hearty breakfast, weighed anchor and sailed to Oak Island Marina where we hauled the boat and painted and varnished til she looked better than she ever had. We were going flat out, me buying charts for all the places we'd be taking the show, Lissa provisioning the boat, getting mattresses recovered, making the domestic scene livable for seven people. Marty was figuring out the rig, getting every line memorized. Davey was learning how to row. François was checking out the engine, changing oil and filters. Bill and Betty were getting things in order at home, packing and arranging to be gone for the summer. Chris was pulling the sound and light system together and getting a van to transport it, since we'd decided that sailing all those electrics might be a tad imprudent.

Our first show was in Annapolis Royal. This meant we had to breast the Fundy tides, the biggest in the world. I studied the "rule of twelfths" and tide tables til it was second nature, and organized the chart table so that the next necessary chart would come to hand without a search. And finally, we were all aboard, Bill and Betty in the forepeak, François in the upper, Marty in the lower, Davey in his hammock, and Lissa and I in the double. Marty's "Tasmanian choke snore" was the source of great humour that first night.

When we cast off that morning, I'm sure none of us knew how big the adventure would be, how great the fun, how hard the work, how deep the friendships would become. But we knew we were doing something wonderful. And we had Lissa to thank for it.

We sailed down the southwestern shore of the province, hard on the wind. I set up a system of watches, we kept to it, and all was well. By nightfall, we were easing the sheets and making the turn at the southern tip of Nova Scotia, bound for the Bay of Fundy. I'd shaped us a course that would take us close to Brier Island, the childhood home of Joshua Slocum, the first man to sail around the world alone. The tides here would be huge, and we had to hit it right. You can't make way against the Fundy tides. They must be slack, or running with you. If you do get it right, you fly. You want to be in deep water with lots of room when they're setting against you.

We got it right, and carried the rising tide from Brier Island all the way into Digby, clearing the gut just before the tide turned. We spent the night at the government wharf in Digby, rafted up to a fishing boat. After dinner, we sang through the show, and the harmonies were becoming close and rich. The next morning, we took on a pilot and made our way upriver to Annapolis Royal and our first show. We'd dressed the boat with signal flags and must have been a grand sight, slipping along past lush farms and fields in the golden summer light. Few cruise the Bay of Fundy because of the tides and it's a real shame. Beauty abounds, and you can learn to work with the tides.

Our first show was a great success, and the theatre in Annapolis Royal was one of the nicest venues on the tour. Lissa sold t-shirts til the last minute and then ran down the dock counting the money as we had to catch the tide immediately after the show, or we'd be hard aground against the dock and miss the next show. Once we were off, heading down the river, I noticed that she was not happy. I couldn't figure why. I heard the dreaded phrase . . . "If you don't know, I'm not telling you." I knew I was in a serious pickle.

Further consultation with the crew wised me up. I'd neglected to give her credit from the stage. The fact that this is never done in the theatre didn't matter. This was our show and we could do what we wanted. She felt that I didn't appreciate all her hard work. That I did appreciate it held no sway and, as I look back on it now, it shouldn't have. She was part of us, and needed to be included in the show. She was from then on, but it took quite a while for her to properly forgive me.

Once down the river, we tied up with the fishing fleet to wait for the tide to turn. It was then we discovered that Junior, Lissa's cat, had jumped ship. I'd asked if anyone had seen him when we left the dock in Annapolis and word was he was in the forepeak. He must have run off at the last minute. Calls were made. Plans were concocted. Tears were shed. The tide turned, and we joined the fishing fleet, like a floating town on the run out through Digby Gut. Junior would have to wait til we got to Margaretsville and our next show.

So it went, from adventure to misadventure, with much laughter and some tears the whole summer long. We sailed no matter what the weather, made every show on time and had more fun than any of us could have wished for. The show got better and better, our management of the boat more and more professional and the only part we didn't like was the two week break we had in the middle. We all missed the foolishness.

What we forged that summer has stood the test of time. Each of us has a special place in the hearts of all of the others. And it gave Lissa and I the courage to marry.

Oh. We found Junior. He was waiting under the dock in Annapolis Royal. He wasn't in a very good mood.

The White Sails crew:
left to right, behind the mast, Marty Reno, Betty Belmore, Chris Beckett, Brian Philips, François Tanguay,
Front, Lissa, Tom, Bill Stevenson

13

Her words came haltingly at first. She was frightened and confused. She had no idea who she was or who I was or what had happened. The nurses put a sign beside the bed. "You are Melissa Gallant. You had a car accident on July 2nd. Your brain was injured. Your husband's name is Tom . . . You live in Stonehurst." That sign gave me the willies. Imagine waking up to one like it. We weren't even sure that she could read it at first. When I was alone, I was haunted by the thought of her waking in the night and trying to understand what had become of her life. I was still trying to figure out what had happened to mine.

Once she was awake, there was more and more help for her. She was visited by a physiotherapist, an occupational therapist and a psychiatrist. All were sympathetic and kind but I remember the occupational therapist especially fondly. She would work with Lissa every day and take hope from the tiniest success. I can still see her working with Lissa's paralyzed hands, holding them, flexing the fingers back and forth ever so gently, fitting them with these strange contraptions with wires and elastic bands to stretch the fingers while she slept. The first time Lissa was able to squeeze her hand, I saw her brush away a tear. Say what you want about the Canadian health care system, but when it works, it's a beautiful thing. If the accident had happened in America, Lissa's home, we'd never have been able to afford the kind of care we got here for free.

Lissa was also visited by the hospital chaplain, a soft-spoken Anglican priest. I'll never forget it. He came into the room and Lissa was propped up in her bed, having just been cleaned up from the supper mess. Her hair was brushed on the good side. Her one eye was open wide.

"Oh Mrs. Gallant," he said, "I was so happy to hear that you're awake. How are you?"

She focused her eye upon him, mustered that lopsided smile and delivered her longest speech to date.

"I'm all fucked up."

I was ever so proud. It put me in mind of Oscar Wilde, on his deathbed in a Paris hotel whose fortunes had been no better than his own. Lord Alfred was there, and some other friends. Near the end, he gazed at the unfortunate wallpaper, turned to those assembled and said with an elegant sigh, "Either that wallpaper goes, or I do."

Death cannot defeat such spirit and our dear Creator must love that kind of talk, after all the earnest prayers.

Our last show was in Louisbourg, and the crew all had places to go and things to do as soon as it was over. This left Lissa and me to sail the boat home by ourselves. So we did. Watches were as long as you could manage. Work was shared without need of negotiation. We had the old girl going along like a schooner should. She's plenty of boat for two in these latitudes. We knew it and were right there with it. She was a happy ship, well provisioned and sailed. We'd had our fights and power struggles and misunderstandings and would again, but we were always at our best when it was the two of us, the

schooner and the sea. The sea has a way of reducing things to the essentials. The essentials, given by life itself through the Maker, are good on the face of it. I remember these times with great happiness.

There were problems with the transmission, which we got worked on in D'Escousse on Isle Madame. I remember we got a little chippy with each other, and had fun begging forgiveness. Then, as we were heading for Halifax, we got caught in a small foggy gale off Larry's River. Sailors from softer places are always surprised that you can have wind and fog. Believe me, you can and it's no fun at all. Our universe was an angry sea shrouded in dense grey fog, cold, damp and ominous. The *terra incognita* of the ancient charts I loved to peruse was just beyond the fog. "Here there be serpents," I said to Lissa as I worked at the charts, keeping us off the rocks that abound in Tor Bay. We could see a boat length, no more. It was a dark night. Lissa was at the helm and I was at the chart table when there was a commotion in the rig. The main peak halyard had let go. I scrambled up on deck, and got the main down and furled as Lissa steered the boat. Then I checked our position and decided we'd sail into Larry's River to find out what had broken, and fix it.

I shaped us a course and went up on deck to trim the sails as Lissa carefully got us on the new heading.

"West by north?"

"West by north . . . for now."

Larry's River is surrounded by rocks and shoals. The air was rich with the smells of land. The fog was thick and the sea was angry. We were going faster than I like to go in such conditions, but we were down to the foresail and needed the power to make her easy to steer in the lumpy seas. I couldn't slow her down and expect Lissa to control her. As I stood there peering into the relentless drear, my ears straining for the sound of water breaking over rocks, my nose sniffing for a whiff too rich with mud and seaweed to be deep water, I prayed. "God, don't hurt this schooner or this woman. Amen." And then, standing there cold and wet and afraid on the bowsprit, *Avenger* booming along in the fog, I added my favourite prayer. "Thanks."

I was where I wanted to be, doing what I wanted to do and my beloved was at the helm and steering a true course. I heard a bell and pointed to it. She gave her a spoke and reached for the fore sheet. The light flashed, dim, beautiful in the grey dark.

I'd never have tried to get in there on such a nasty night if we hadn't been in just weeks before. Both of us could remember the entrance. So with Lissa at the helm and me on the bow, we sailed into the tiny port and tied up at the wharf. We were cold, wet and tired, and very happy with ourselves. We'd handled the whole thing without a raised voice beyond the necessary shouting down the wind. We were a fine schooner crew, the two of us.

So we lit the lamps, cooked a hot meal, poured rum in our enameled tin cups and the world was a fine place to be.

"I'd sail anywhere with you, Lissa. You're steady at the helm and brave when things get gnarly."

"All I did was steer."

"Right. In half a gale, in the fog on a black night, by the compass. Not many I'd trust with that job."

"Really?"

"Steering by the compass is hard and you know it. And we had no margin for error." I raised my cup in a toast. "Here's to the best schooner sailor from Tennessee with big hair in the world."

And we clinked our cups and drank. Then Lissa looked at me.

"You still serious about getting married?"

"Be a shame not to after I've asked you so many times. We could sail to the Caribbean for the honeymoon."

"What about money?"

"Better to starve where it's warm."

And so, as we sailed home to Mahone Bay, Lissa and I decided that we should get married. In my mind, I had done everything necessary, and the wedding would now be arranged and all I would have to do was rent a tux and turn up. But times were changing and Lissa had other ideas. We would not be "churched" in Tennessee. The whole thing would happen in Nova Scotia, and I would arrange it. Oh.

There was no manual for this kind of thing. I started asking everyone I knew if they knew someone who could perform a marriage. The usual answer was a minister or priest, which was what I was afraid of, given my solitary spiritual meanderings at the time. I phoned this parish and that.

"Are you a member of our congregation?"

"No."

"Well, I'd like to help but . . . "

Prevailing opinion was that the Unitarians would be a good bet, but they were booked solid. I was getting desperate. We had decided to sail to the Caribbean for the winter no matter what the financial situation, and were hauled out at Oak Island Marina to give the boat a coat of tropical bottom paint to protect her from the teredo worms. One evening there was a big party at the yard. Among the guests was Judge Peter Nicholson, a prominent retired cabinet minister. He had an eye for the ladies and spent a long time talking to Lissa. He obviously found her company invigorating.

I cornered the good judge later in the evening and asked if he could perform marriages.

"Yes, but I won't. I don't agree with marriage."

"Shame. I was hoping you'd do one for me."

"Who's the woman?"

"You were talking to her. She's right over there."

He looked at Lissa, then back at me.

"All right. Just this once."

And so it was arranged. I made a few phone calls, and the folks I called made a few phone calls and the following Sunday at noon the judge steamed into the marina in his own wooden boat. I caught his lines, he came aboard *Avenger* and the ceremony was performed on the foredeck, which was bedecked with flowers and flags and crowded with friends from everywhere. My sister Cathy and brother-in-law Michael stood for us. After the vows, which the judge had altered to read "love, honour and humour one another," with which we heartily agreed, we went below to sign the papers. Came the moment when he looked up from the form, pen in hand and asked . . .

"Religion?"

"Pagan," I said. He wrote it in large block letters with a joyous smile.

There are those dear to me who think there was blasphemy, even damnation, in that word. Pagan. Truth told, it was all I could think of at that instant, since I'm not a joiner where the immortal mysteries are concerned. I just blurted it out. But now that I think about it, as near as I can tell, a pagan believes that everything is God; every rock and tree and star in the sky and winter gale and summer breeze and new potato and old woman and Buddha-like baby and mad whirling medicine man and prophet and song and story and

holy book and the Cross of sacrifice which is the essence of love and nothing is excluded and there's no way to go to hell but to willfully go to hell.

I declare myself Christian because I believe the story of the cross but I don't believe that there is only one way to salvation. It doesn't stand to reason. When I pray, it is most often to Jesus. My King James Bible is well thumbed and deeply treasured. So are books about Buddha, and the Baha'i teachings and the Koran, the Tao and Zen masters, the poets, the storytellers, the singers and the songs, the wisdom of foolishness. All of the holy books are a continuing poem addressed to the great mystery. Why are we here? All of the great faiths contain wisdom and truth. All of them try to make us understand that love is life and death holds no dominion where love is known, sought with an eager heart. All of them mean to help us succeed at being happy when we can and brave in time of tragedy. So why all the holy wars? How can such a phrase even exist?

Is it because all religions are degraded by human interpretation, especially the lunatic fundamentalists? They are certainly degraded by my meagre attempts at understanding. And most of them claim to be the one true path and insist upon an act of faith that defies reason, and furthermore, deny salvation to the uninitiated. This is cruel and wrong if God is love, and what other definition bears scrutiny? I said "pagan" in answer to the judge's question. In my mind, pagan isn't a religion. It's a description of a frame of mind. Everything is holy and each of us is part of an eternal whole that we can begin to understand if we'll only shut up and listen. I'm down with that. I'm going to heaven, or die trying.

There was a large crowd of good friends, a huge potluck banquet and the party went on for hours. The entire cost for the production was the judge's fee. A bottle of gin. Good gin. Green bottle. Forty ouncer.

14

ONE MORNING I WALKED INTO THE ROOM and Lissa's bed was empty. I was startled. She couldn't walk. The bathroom was empty. Had they taken her for some kind of test? Was she all right? Fighting back a rush of panic, I went looking for a nurse and found Lissa sitting in a big chair with small wheels and a table across her lap, parked near the nurses' station. She was painstakingly turning the pages of a magazine. She looked lost and sad. She hadn't noticed me so I watched her for a few moments. I don't know what she was seeing on those pages. She turned them, looked for a few moments, then turned again. She had the aspect of a child being punished for acting up in class. She was doing what she was told but there was no heart in it.

"Hi Lissa."

She looked up, startled, and burst into tears. She was still surprised when I appeared, even though I came every day.

"Oh . . . oh . . . I'm so glad you came . . . "

"They got you up."

"I don't know what I'm supposed to be doing."

"I guess they just wanted to give you a change of scenery."

"They just left me here. I don't know why. I don't . . . "

She was crying and then indignant. When she got angry, there were no governors on it so I had to head it off at the pass.

"Do you want to go back to your room?"

"Yes. It has a window."

I gathered up a few more magazines and stacked them on her little table, wheeled the contraption back into her room and parked it by the window. I sat on the bed beside her. It was a sunny day.

"You must be glad to be out of bed for a change."

"I thought, if you came, you wouldn't be able to find me."

Tears again.

"I'll always find you. I'm getting to know my way around this place."

"Why do you come? I'm no good. I can't think. I can't do anything."

"Don't say things like that, Lissa. You're brave and strong and you're getting better. It's just going to take some time."

"But I can't remember your name and I don't know why you come."

"My name is Tom. I'm your husband. I come because I love you."

❦

WE WERE ANCHORED IN PRINCE'S INLET, in Mahone Bay, fully provisioned and waiting for a "window" in the weather to sail to Bermuda. Aboard were Lissa and I, Marty and Gypsy Dave, and our charter guest, Al Brideau, the world's oldest hippie. Al had come to hippiedom late, and lived with the fervent passion of the convert. He had no time at all for "straight society." He fit right in but was a pure landlubber on a steep learning curve. Davey loved to take him around the boat and "show him the ropes." Al took the lessons seriously.

We were all excited about our first big ocean passage, listening to the weather four times a day, watching the sky and the barometer. We were sailing in company with another schooner, Corky Wood's *Buccaneer Prince*. She'd made the passage many times and we were glad of the company. Every day, Corky and I would confer about the weather. The thing is to wait out the hurricanes and then run for it before the winter gales set in. It's a nice theory. Fact is, sailing to Bermuda in the fall is a chancy proposition at best. Above thirty degrees of latitude the weather can change in a heartbeat, with cold fronts rolling across the continent and funneling out across the sea between Cape Hatteras and Newfoundland. They all seem to meet between Nova Scotia and Bermuda.

And then there's the Gulf Stream, a river of fast-moving warm water in the middle of the passage that's a weather factory. Where warm meets cold, you've got trouble. So we were edgy and worked at staying busy and keeping things light. The time between finishing with provisioning and casting off is often the hardest part of the voyage. I've had crew arrive excited and ready and then leave the boat before the voyage began because they couldn't take the pressure of anticipation. But we were ready for the ocean. We'd been sailing together all summer (except for Al) and knew one another and the boat. Davey was a great distraction. He conceived of our destination as a place called "Down South." He was full of questions.

"Lissa, is Down South really warm all the time?"

"It sure is. And there's palm trees and golden beaches and turquoise water."

"And naked women." This from Marty, with a wink.

"Really, Lissa?"

"Well, Davey, I'm sure some folks do take their clothes off when they're alone, to sunbathe. But your dad and Cap'n Tom tend to exaggerate things."

"Marty, do you know why Lissa insists on making light of our extensive research of Down South?"

"Search me, Cap. You'd think she'd be thankful we checked things out."

"It's a good thing Davey has me. You two'd have him ruined for good in a week."

"Don't worry, Lissa. I know when they're funnin' me."

"I'll bet you do. They're not hard to figure out."

I was sewing a ditty bag for my rigging tools. Marty was making a rigger's bucket. Lissa was stowing and restowing things and cooking feast upon feast. Al was practicing knots and reading. And every evening, after supper, we'd take turns reading to Davey from *Charlotte's Web*. We were all captivated by the spider and the pig and cried harder than Davey at the end.

There was also a daily trip to town for more fresh food to replenish what we'd eaten and to get more ice. *Avenger* didn't have a fridge back then, or a shower, so every few days there was a shower run. We stayed as busy as we could, but still, each day held time for private thoughts about the voyage ahead. I don't think any of us feared for our lives. We knew we had a good boat and that we knew how to sail her. I was concerned about navigation. We had a Loran C, but that would become less and less reliable as we got further offshore. I could take a sextant fix, but was new to it. We had a good compass and a "Walker Rocket" log and all the necessary charts. Dead reckoning was our ace in the hole. If you know where you started from, the direction you're going and your average speed, you know where you are. Not exactly. There are tides and currents to take into account, but if you stay on the chart, you're never lost.

Bermuda is a tiny low archipelago in the middle of a big ocean. It's surrounded by dangerous reefs and can only be approached safely from the east. I spent a lot of time going over the charts, reading the pilot books. Lissa would look over my shoulder, asking questions. Then she'd make lemon muffins.

And there were other things to conjure on. After Davey was asleep, we'd sit up and talk over a rum or two. We were leaving the world we knew behind. Al was all in favour.

"Nothing to hold me here. I was a good citizen, worked hard, wore suits, made money. What for? None of it made any sense when you figure you're gonna die and you spent most of your life under fluorescent lights in an ugly room doing something stupid. I hate fluorescent lights!"

"Not a patch on a kerosene lamp."

"Or the sun."

"Or the moon."

Lissa raised her glass.

"Gentlemen . . . the moon."

And we clinked, emptied our cups, recharged them.

"It's funny how things happen," Marty said. "Me 'n' Dave were lost when we walked down the dock looking for *Avenger*. We just wanted a friendly face to talk to. We found a job, a new family and a new life."

"We needed you, Marty."

"Really, you guys. The way you took us in, the way you are with Davey . . . "

"Davey's the best thing about this summer."

"Lissa, you'll never know what you're giving him. He lost his mother . . . not forever . . . but for now. He was sad when he came aboard. Now he's happy."

"He was some quiet at first. Didn't say two words til he told you where the flashlight was. That's when I knew we had us a sailor."

"Gentlemen," said Lissa. "The Cabin Boy."

"The dirty little nipper," quoth all, and there was more clinking and drinking.

So it went, as front after front passed through and we watched the sky. Lissa's birthday was October 22. We decided that a celebration was in order. So, the night before, we waited for her to fall asleep, and I baked a cake while we plotted the next morning's festivities. We'd wake her with the cake, candles alight, all of us naked and singing. Figured that would get a laugh.

It did.

15

EVERY DAY NOW, I'd find Lissa in the strange high-backed chair near the nurses' station, thumbing through magazines. Every day, she'd see me and burst into tears.

"Oh . . . oh . . . I thought you wouldn't come."

To be greeted every morning with tears of joy is a rare gift. There were challenges and sorrows in every visit, but always, I was buoyed up by Lissa's passionate response to my arrival. After that, all bets were off. I was hypersensitive to any sign of healing or its opposite. Brain injuries cause such devastation in so many unexpected ways that it often feels like two steps forward, one step back. One day she'd know my name, the next she wouldn't.

I decided one morning that it was time to get her out of the hospital. If she could sit in the strange high-backed chair, she could sit in a wheelchair. So I got one from the nurses, got her dressed for going out and with much "oh . . . oh . . . I can't . . . " managed the journey to the elevator. As we waited for it to come, she asked,

"Where are you taking me?"

"You'll see."

"You're taking me to the barn to beat me and leave me with the pigs."

"No barns in Halifax."

The elevator arrived, and soon I wheeled her out into the golden September light. There were more tears. Then, once she'd settled down, we started away from the hospital. I was taking her to the Public Gardens, one of the treasures of Halifax. A full city block in size, it's an old and well cared for Victorian botanical garden with winding paths, fountains and ponds, exotic trees and flowers. And ducks. The ducks were our destination. We'd always shared an affection for ducks.

As I wheeled her along the sidewalk, I began to notice the eyes of passers-by. Women, especially the well dressed ones, seemed unable to give her more than a furtive sidelong glance. Men were different. They'd look at her, nod, say "good day" or something. She was still obviously very badly hurt. She had trouble holding her head up, and only half a hairdo. I was used to the way she was, and seeing the response of strangers was a difficult reminder of how far we had to go.

As I pushed her through the wrought iron gates of the garden, she pulled herself together. Her head came erect, her eye opened wide and she was alive to the surroundings.

"Oh . . . oh . . . thank you. Look at the flowers . . . the birds . . . "

I wheeled her through the park slowly, stopping now and then so she could look at whatever caught her fancy. Occasionally she'd remember the name of a flower, one that I didn't know.

"Look . . . look . . . " and then the name. "Is that right? How do I know that?"

"Your parents had a flower shop."

"They did? Oh . . . I think I remember that."

I could tell she didn't. It's torture watching a brain trying to heal itself. There are bursts of memory like the flowers and then great big blank spots like the shop. You can never be sure that things are really getting better. It's all so random.

There's a big pond in the middle of the garden that's full of ducks. Lissa lit up when she saw it. I parked the wheelchair by the pond, and gave her bag of corn that I'd brought for the occasion. She was beside herself. She threw some corn. The ducks were on it in a flash. Soon, there were dozens of ducks around the chair and she was feeding them, trying to make them behave. When one duck was being left out of the feast, she would ache for it, trying to throw some kernels its way.

"Here ducky, ducky . . . here . . . see it . . . oh. Why is that one so slow?"

"All ducks are not created equal, I guess."

"At least she wasn't hit by a bus."

When the corn was gone, she said goodbye to the ducks and we rolled on. I had another stop planned. On the way to the Gardens, alongside Victoria Park, I'd noticed a chip wagon that featured fresh cut fries. The perfect antidote to hospital food. I bought Lissa a large order, laced it with salt and ketchup as per her instructions and we found a quiet spot under a tree for the feast. She was in heaven and making a glorious mess, ketchup from stem to stern. I had to make two trips back to the wagon to get more napkins.

I took the long way back to the hospital and grew less self-conscious about the way people looked at her. I got defiant and proud of my ketchup-spattered date. When the hospital finally came into view . . .

"Oh no. Do we have to go back?"

"I'm sorry, Lissa. The O.T. comes today. But we'll go out again. I promise."

"I loved the ducks."

She was crying when we got on the elevator.

WE WERE FINISHING OUR BREAKFAST of birthday cake and coffee when Corky came alongside.

"Now or never, Cap."

"Yeah. The weather didn't sound too bad this morning and the glass is up."

"Cold front over Hudson Bay bound this way. We leave now, we'll probably outrun it. We don't leave now, we'll have to wait it out. Could take another week."

"We'll make an ice run and we're ready. When should we leave?"

"Soon's you're ready. Noonish?"

"Sounds good.

It was a beautiful day. Blue skies, big fat cumulus clouds. No reason to worry. We set to getting the last bits stowed, sent Al for ice, took off the sail covers and Lissa made a big pot of stew and a pan of muffins for the first twenty-four hours. We were ready to go.

The charts were organized. I flashed up the Loran C, set up the Walker Rocket on the stern. It's an ancient instrument that my uncle John had given me. It works by trailing a rocket shaped spinner at the end of a long line over the stern. It turns as it moves through the water and the instrument at the other end of the line logs the miles travelled. I checked the sextant for error, got out some work sheets. Then I listened to the weather again. No mention of the cold front yet. (We knew about it because Corky was watching the weather on television.) That meant it was still well inland. Nowadays, the weather forecasting is much more sophisticated and you can get five day offshore forecasts on the internet.

Al returned with the ice. Corky's crew was aboard *Buccaneer Prince*. We raised the anchor, stowed it in the forepeak and dogged down the hatch. We were bound for Bermuda.

We steamed out of the inlet together, and raised sail as soon as things opened up a little. We tucked a single reef in the main, and then raised the fore, jumbo and jib. The course for Bermuda is due south, true. The wind was from the nor'west. Things were looking good. We were booming along with all sheets eased, right on the rhumb line.

For the next two days, all was well. The wind continued from the nor'west and we sailed along our course. The sea makes relentless demands on the voyager. You're constantly moving. Every simple act is more difficult. Making coffee. Going to the bathroom – the head. It takes a couple of days to get your legs. When you finally do, the passage could last forever. Unless you are subject to *mal de mer*. Lissa gets seasick, but she's brave in the face of it. No matter what, she always stood her watch. At sea, I do all the cooking. I don't get seasick but claim no glory for the fact. Just luck. But it does mean I can work down below when things get lumpy. And lumpy they were by the end of the second day.

And they were bound to get lumpier. We were closing on the Gulf Stream, and the combination of wind from the north and current from the south always makes for tough sledding. Lissa was existing on little yellow plums that were the only thing she could keep down. The wind was piping up. Marty and Dave have stomachs like mine and were having fun. Al was a little under the weather, and he and Lissa were working on a comedy duo based on the fine art of puking over the side without getting any on the boat or yourself. All in all, everything was under control.

The barometer was steady. But there was less and less blue in the sky. After day one, getting a sun sight was a matter of luck. The wind was slowly building, and moving to the north. I was starting to worry, having heard more than enough yarns about nor'easters in the Gulf Stream. But nothing radical ever happened. It just built . . . slowly. And when the boat started dipping her deadeyes, we'd reef. If you've never sailed deep water, you can't ever know the majesty of the seas. They roll for hundreds of miles, and until they start breaking, they're not a problem – they're a wonder. But they are big.

I was standing the midnight watch on our third night out when I heard something unusual from the foredeck. I got the flashlight and checked things out. The pin that holds the fore gooseneck had sheared off and the fore boom was running amok. It had to be secured. I called Lissa and Marty. She was dressed and on deck in a flash. Marty wasn't far behind. I explained the situation.

"The fore boom is out of the gooseneck . . . you know, where that shaft on the boom goes into the socket on the mast fitting. The wind is driving it forward. We have to get it back, and jam another pin in there."

"Jesus," said Lissa. "Got a pin?"

"Here. Good thing I sewed that ditty bag. Knew right where it was."

"How do we do it?"

"Marty steers. You and I go up there, you to the foremast, me to the mainmast end of the boom. I'll haul it back, and then you jam it down into the socket and pin it."

"Sure. Make me go out on the bow."

"Figure you can haul it back?"

"A joke, Cappy."

"Oh. Right. How obtuse of me. Shall we commence to risk our lives?"

"Guys," said Marty, all serious. "It's been real."

Grinning all, we went to work. It was dark. There was plenty of spray coming aboard forward but it was warm. We were in the Stream. It was howling. Lissa and I worked our way to our places, got set up. Now we had to shout.

"You ready?"

"Wait. I have to get the pin."

I could just see her, shifting her weight, digging into her foul weather jacket, watching the seas, ducking when necessary. She was magnificent. She found the pin, set herself up with a good purchase on the boom, looked at me. I grabbed the foresail bail and gave it a mighty tug.

"Jesus. It's a hard pull. On three."

She nodded. I braced my feet on the hatch, put my back in it.

"One . . . two . . . three . . . " I hauled til veins were popping, she pulled it into place, rammed the shaft into the socket and cursed and swore, trying to get the pin in place. I scampered to her, got a flashlight on it and between us, we did the job, and then made our way back to the cockpit. We were booming along in big seas. Marty looked at us as if we were back from the dead.

"Does this mean I have to give the boat back?"

Marty and Dave.

16

WHEN THE BUS HIT US, *Avenger* was still hauled up on the land with one coat of bottom paint on her. Except for moments of worry as I drove home from the hospital to feed the cats and check on the house, I hadn't been able to give her any attention. But she tugged at my heart. She's mahogany planked, and if she stands ashore for too long, the planks dry and shrink, opening the seams so she leaks for a while before they swell up again after launching.

Many's the wise one has cautioned against becoming too attached to physical things, and for the most part, my affection for any of the stuff I've acquired over the years has been well placed, glad to have it while I did, but able to suffer its loss with equanimity. This does not extend to the schooner. David Stevens, who designed and built her, was given to saying that "A boat is the nearest thing to a living being that a man can create with his hands." This is precisely why she has such a strong call on my heart and why I would suffer her loss like that of a dear friend.

We have sailed so far together. She has taught me so much about myself and the world around me that I can barely imagine life without her. I am inclined to living inside my head.

Avenger insists that I notice the outside world. I am inclined to sitting and thinking, daydreaming, staring out the window. *Avenger* gets me up and going, returns me to my physical self and keeps me in shape. She has taught me to be a rigger and a deep water sailor, and how to operate a chisel and a plane. She has forced me to learn the workings of the marine diesel engine. Because of her, I see the sky with new eyes and always know the phases of the moon. Where I was fearful, she has made me brave; where I was vain, she has made me humble. She asks a lot in the way of care and attention, but gives as much and more in return. She is a lesson I needed to learn.

Now I was neglecting her, for the best of reasons, but it bothered me. If I could just get her in the water, I could sail her to Halifax and have a place to live while I took care of Lissa. Enter friends. Chris Reardon, who'd sailed with me from my early days with *Avenger*, rounded up some hands and they finished the painting and got her ready to launch. I had no idea they were doing this. I'd had a new set of masts made for her, and they got them hauled to the yard and ready to step. Once she was ready, I got a call from Chris. In his quiet, dry way he suggested that maybe we'd better get the old girl wet before she turned into a potato chip.

"She needs a lot of work and I'm not sure I'll be able to do it."

"Tide'll be high around eleven on Saturday," said Chris. "We need you to check the rigging on the new masts."

"Oh." I was beginning to realize what he was saying. I was thunderstruck. "Chris . . . "

"See you Saturday."

And so it was. I arrived at the yard to be greeted by *Avenger* looking all shiny and new and a crew of the kind of friends that make life tolerable, even sweet. We launched her, stepped the masts, bent on the sails and sailed her to Mahone Bay, flying a pennant from the mainmast provided by Chris. A blue pennant with bright yellow letters that said "Lizzy."

Lizzy was what we called Lissa aboard the boat. I think Davey had started it. I'd made up a little song:

High seas Lizzy with the golden hair,
Suntanned beauty with a life to share.
She's a ship that's sailing everywhere.
Love's the wind and life's the sea,
And we're the craziest family . . .

Chris had also been one of the most constant visitors at the hospital. He'd stop in every other evening and just sit with Lissa, not saying much. Chris never says much, and when he does more often than not, it's an astringent barb, a prick to the balloon of overweening self. I knew him for years before I realized that he was joking and these barbs were the currency of his affection. How many relationships come adrift because the one cannot accept the currency of the other's caring?

We got a big break at the hospital when a private room became available, and the kind nurses gave it to us. Over and over again you'll hear that the nurses are the heroes of the health care system. They are, and are overworked and underpaid. Once in the private room, we were free to be ourselves, such as we were. Lissa was lost in confusion most of the time. But there were moments of clarity that were breathtaking. One evening, Lennie Gallant, the wonderful songwriter and an old shipmate, was visiting and we were talking about a film he'd just seen. He'd liked it but was put off by the callow presence of the leading man.

"These young actors . . . they just don't seem to have the depth of previous generations. I never believed the guy was in trouble."

"I know what you mean," I said. "There's something lacking. Hard to figure what it is."

Lissa looked at us with her one eye.

"They've never had the blues."

Ever so stealthily, the gale in the Gulf Stream had become a full on storm. We were down to the deep reefed foresail, running in front of it. I was at the helm and we were going like hell, making in excess of ten knots against the current. A big sea rose up behind me. I could feel *Avenger* lifting, and then just as it reached us, it broke and we were lifted on a maelstrom of white water. *Avenger* was surfing, going twice her hull speed, the bow-wave all the way back to the main shrouds. It was thrilling and completely mad. We had to slow her down, or so I thought at the time. Now, I'd be inclined to keep her going as long as we both could stand it. I'd shorten sail, but I wouldn't stop her.

I'd never tried "laying a-hull" before. It's a recognized storm tactic. You take all the sail off, batten everything down and leave the boat to her own resources. On some boats, like double enders that have no overhangs astern to pound in the seaway, this seems to work. Not on *Avenger*. We lay below, trying to rest. Seas would break down on her like cannons. She'd shudder and shake them off. The only one who wasn't bothered by the fury of it all was Davey. He'd set himself up on the cabin floor with his matchbox cars. When the boat rose to a sea, he'd let them go and they'd race across the cabin, only to race back to him as she rolled back the other way. As he played this game, he sang "Rudolph, The Red-Nosed Reindeer," to the deep amusement of all. After an hour or so of crashing and banging, I decided that this was no way to treat a lady, and we suited up, went back on deck, gave her the reefed jumbo and steered for Bermuda. Wild as it was, it was better than just taking the blows.

The worst part of the storm had some real legs, and lasted about thirty-six hours. I shortened watches to an hour on, three off, because steering required so much attention, and the white noise of the wind and sea took such a toll on our spirits. It was relentless and almost unbearable after dark. It was a strange storm, big and wild but with no real fall in the barometer. It had dropped a couple of tenths, but nothing serious.

The worst of the wind left us as it had come, slowly enough that it took us a while to believe that conditions were improving. Then it veered to the south, and gained enough strength to make us heave her to. Now, with the helm lashed and the reefed foresail, we could rest as *Avenger* jogged to windward slowly, steering herself. With the wind now blowing with the Gulf Stream, the seas moderated and became long swells that no longer broke down on us. It was just a matter of waiting it out, hoping for a shift that would let us go where we wanted to. And since we didn't have to steer, we made a good hot meal and got some rest. Standing watch was just a matter of sweeping the horizon every ten minutes or so, looking for ships.

The sky was beginning to open up. The full moon was visible now and then, and more and more stars appeared, giving me hope that soon I'd get a fix with the sextant. The batteries were low (turned out we'd been sold a dud in Lunenburg), too low to start the engine, and I'd turned off all the electrics to give them a chance to come back a little. I wanted the VHF radio when we neared Bermuda. If I couldn't get a fix, it was dead reckoning to a reef-strewn island. Lissa was concerned.

"How can you be sure we won't hit the reefs?"

"Well, I can't, but what I'm doing now is making the boat bigger in my mind. Right now she's about four miles wide and all the extra beam is to the west."

"That makes sense. What about the Gulf Stream?"

"I think we'll be out of it by morning, and it's setting us to the east which is what we want."

We were standing over the chart table. The moon was full and Al was on watch, blissed out by the appearance of the moon and stars. We could hear him oohing and ahing.

"I always liked the sound of the Gulf Stream," Lissa said. "Something romantic about it. But now that we're in it, I have to say that the Gulf Stream is no friend of mine."

"You'll get no argument from me. You should get some sleep. You're on after me."

"Are we close to Bermuda?"

"I've got us right here." I pointed to an x on the chart. "If we get a westerly shift, which is what I think it's doing, we should get there tomorrow."

"I trust you, Tom."

"We'll see."

Lissa crawled into our berth and I made a fresh pot of coffee. Al continued his rhapsodic exclamations, talking to the stars and moon. I climbed into my foul weather gear and asked Al how things were on deck.

"Beautiful . . . magnificent. I'm dry, Cappy, and the sky is full of stars."

"I'll be right up."

As I poured myself a mug of coffee, I heard the telltale hiss of a wave, and then the crash as it dumped fifty gallons on Al's dry head. There were no more joyous exclamations. He was silent as I relieved him. I watched from the cockpit as he stood in the galley and removed his sodden gear, found his towel and dried off. Then he found the rum, had a deep pull on the bottle and crawled into his berth.

I looked at the stars, patches of them between the clouds. You'd need to be quick to get a sight. I decided to wait for the sun. Then I heard Al stirring. He was at the sink, naked, filling a large glass with water. There was a dark fury in his countenance. He climbed up into the cockpit, fixed the sea with a flinty gaze and threw the water at it.

"There," quoth the naked mariner. "Now we're even."

And he went to bed. My watch passed quickly, what with the laughing and all.

17

I don't remember sailing to Halifax that autumn of 1992. You'd think I would. I was homesick for the boat, aching to go back to sea, and the fear was growing in me that all of that was over, forever. Lissa was so hurt, and healing so slowly. On the rare occasions that I let myself look at the horizon, all I could see was her face, that one good eye full of fear and confusion. Beyond that face loomed the tax audit and sure financial ruin. The future bore no scrutiny. I had to content myself with the present. Any other cast of mind disabled me completely.

I do remember waking up with the sunrise at the wharf of the Maritime Museum of the Atlantic. On the boat, I'm an early riser. On land, I can sleep around the clock. I made a pot of strong coffee, sat in the cockpit and watched as the city stirred itself. The ferry from Dartmouth scurried back and forth across the harbour bearing its cargo of commuters. Some brisk, some bleary-eyed, some well turned out, some dowdy, at first a trickle and then a river, they walked along the waterfront, cardboard cups of coffee in hand, and were swallowed up by the highrises that march up the hill like transplants from Toronto.

I went below and busied myself with housekeeping chores. It's a comforting ritual. Make up your berth, sweep the cabin floor, wipe down the table and countertops, wash the dishes. Always, as you're doing this, little jobs come to mind. Every boat, properly loved, has lists.

"I should make a shelf for the alarm clock . . . that mast boot needs snugging up . . . should take the jack plane to that door . . . the gaff saddles need new leather . . . "

All of these things that need doing do not oppress the sailor's heart. They bring comfort and a sense of purpose. If the boat is in good condition, you know you're living well. A sailor is a care giver for the vessel that bears him on the wide impartial ocean. If he isn't, the ocean will swallow them both.

At ten, I made the climb up the hill through the centre of downtown Halifax to the hospital. I stopped at a coffee shop on Spring Garden Road and bought a cappuccino and croissant for Lissa on the way. I walked at a brisk pace, and was winded by the time I reached the glass doors of the hospital. My smoker chum with the funny housecoat gave me a nod as I caught my breath. I contemplated sharing a smoke with him, but was shamed out of it by my huffing and puffing.

Lissa received me with exclamations and tears as always, and I wheeled her back to her room and gave her the coffee and croissant. She loved it.

"Remember St. Barth's, Lissa? We were anchored off the ruins of the old hospital. Speedy John was anchored right beside us in *Aldee*. I used to go ashore every morning and get fresh croissants from the little *boulangerie*. You and Davey loved the ones with chocolate filling."

She struggled to remember but was drawing a blank and it made her sad. I tried to comfort her.

"It's ok, Lissa. Last week you couldn't remember my name. Now you do."

"Before you came this morning, I tried to remember your name and whether you said you were coming today. I couldn't. I was lonesome and afraid."

She was weeping, her grief ungoverned by social convention.

"But I'll always be here. I come every day."

"If you didn't, I don't know if I'd remember."

"You're getting better. I can see it even if you can't. Eat your croissant."

She pulled herself together and purposefully consumed the croissant, sipping the cappuccino after each bite. As I watched, I'd have given anything to know what was going on in her injured brain. She looked childlike, focused on the job of eating and drinking, lost in it. Every little gesture took an act of will. Raise the cup to the mouth, open the mouth, tip the cup, sip the coffee, swallow carefully, return the cup to the table. Raise the croissant . . . There were moments of danger for her in all of it. Swallowing was difficult and she was prone to terrible bouts of choking. She'd learned an elaborate swallowing protocol. She'd take the bite, or sip, lower her chin, swallow, raise her chin a little, swallow again. When she finished, she looked up and was almost surprised to see me there.

"Are we married?"

"Yes, for our sins."

"You poor man."

"Don't say that, Lissa. I'm not complaining."

"You should. I'm no good anymore. I can't think. I can't even walk."

"Don't . . . "

"Nobody deserves this . . . " and she dissolved into tears again. I tried to put my arms around her. She pushed me away, flailing at me full of fury, again ungoverned. Her anger was monumental, out of control. I stood back, on the verge of tears myself. She'd scratched my cheek and it was bleeding.

"Go away!"

"Lissa . . . "

"Leave me alone. Leave me . . . "

"I'll be back after lunch."

I stopped at the nurses' station and told them that if Lissa got worried about where I was, I was going for lunch and would be back in a couple of hours. The nurse looked at me.

"How are you bearing up?"

"Day at a time. She's getting better."

"Don't forget to take some time for yourself."

"That's what I'm doing right now."

"A couple of hours isn't enough. You'll burn yourself out if you don't take some time away from all this."

"I will when I can. Don't worry."

I bought a medium order of home cut fries from the chip wagon, loaded them with malt vinegar and salt and walked to the Public Gardens. I shared my chips with Lissa's ducks, taking care to lob some to the timid stragglers.

"Don't be timid, ducks. To the brave goes the fries."

A very pretty girl watched me for a moment. Our eyes met. She smiled. There was a tender moment, I turned back to the ducks and she was gone when I looked back her way. As the ducks and I finished the fries I wondered if one so young and beautiful had ever been touched by tragedy.

I wondered if she'd believe that the scratches on my cheek were fencing scars that I'd acquired in a duel fought that morning on a dew-covered meadow.

THE SUN ROSE A WAN WASHED-OUT YELLOW and my spirits were lifted. No "red sky at morning, sailor take warning." The sea was rolling still, but had organized itself. The clouds had moved up some and were mostly cumulus. There were a couple of big ones on the horizon, contemplating becoming line squalls. The wind was holding from the south, and my hoped-for westerly shift wasn't happening. The opposite was. We were going to have to claw to windward if we were to make Bermuda that day, and the foresail wasn't going to do it for us. We needed to drop it and replace it with the reefed main, jumbo and jib. As the foresail came down, Al let the peak halyard go, and it ended up running through the block aloft and falling on the deck. This meant we no longer had the foresail as an option. Not a problem if the wind stayed where it was.

With the new combination of sails, *Avenger* set to work, breasting the seas with a bone in her teeth. She romped along, helm lashed, with a contrite Al on watch, as I worked at the charts. We were out of the Gulf Stream so the easterly set was not an issue. I figured we'd made no more than twenty miles through the night and were about sixty miles to the north of the middle of Bermuda. We were on the starboard tack, and headed southeast by east. If I was right, we were in good shape to make Town Cut before dark. If I was wrong, it was imperative that I err to the east. The Bermuda charts are full of warnings about compass anomalies and shifting sands and currents. I got out the sextant and hoped for a couple of sun sights.

I made a fresh pot of coffee and a big breakfast. Everyone was up and excited, since today was the day we'd make our landfall. I hoped. I tried to keep my nerves under wraps as I served bacon and eggs to everyone.

"Should we keep a lookout, Cap'n Tom?" Davey was eager to get a look at "Down South."

"Not yet. Bermuda's notoriously hard to see and we're still a ways off."

"Queer place to put an island," said Marty. "Right out in the middle of the ocean."

"Ain't that the truth."

"Look . . . rainbows!"

Davey was right. There were five of them, big bright rainbows arching across the sky. And then, like a ghost from another time, a square-rigger off the port bow, topsails braced and bound to the east sou'east.

"Holy doodle," said Davey. "Pirates!"

"No question about it. All hands prepare for battle!"

She was no more than ten miles off and obviously bound for Bermuda. I took the lashing off the wheel and steered a course that would bring us up alongside her. I gave the helm to Lissa and went below to the charts. I wanted to have our assumed position ready when I talked to her skipper. Then I turned on the VHF, hoping the batteries had built back up enough.

Back in the cockpit, all were transfixed by the vision of the ancient ship. We were drawing closer, and could now see that she was made of wood and authentic in every way. Her sails were patched, her topsides scarred. Her motion was majestic as she lifted to the long seas. She was the *Regina Maris*, one of the last wooden square-riggers still making a living on the sea. She was operated as a school ship/research vessel out of Woods Hole, Massachusetts.

"Schooner, schooner, schooner, *Regina Maris*."

I lept below and grabbed the radio mic.

"*Regina Maris*, Schooner *Avenger*, over."

"*Avenger*. Where are you coming from, and where bound? Over."

"*Regina Maris*, we're from Lunenburg and bound for Bermuda. You?"

"Out of Woods Hole."

We talked about the storm, and then I gave him our assumed position and asked if he could verify it. He asked me to stand by.

"*Avenger . . . Regina Maris*. You're a few miles east of your position. Allowing for error, were you? Over."

"Trying to stay off Kitchen Shoals. I had the boat four miles wide."

"Good plan. We're bound through Town Cut, over."

"Mind if we tag along? Over."

"Glad for the company, Cap. See you at the White Horse."

So my anxieties eased and we sailed along together. We took pictures of them, they took pictures of us. We were in a bubble out of time, both boats carrying rigs of ancient design, both built of wood in the old way. As we closed on the island, we sailed into the grandmother of all squalls, black and fierce, with rain so thick that we could barely see *Regina Maris* when we knew she was no more than two hundred yards away. I was very glad she had radar. We strained to keep her in sight until the squall eased up. When it did, there it was. Bermuda.

We were about four miles to the east of Town Cut. The wind came east after the squall, so we could reach back and forth while we waited for *Regina Maris* to make her way into St. George's Harbour. I listened as they made contact with Bermuda Harbour Radio, one of the best such services in the world. They were cleared to enter Town Cut. Then I called and explained that we couldn't use our engine and would sail in. The radio operator didn't like the sound of that, and suggested that we get a tow. I asked about prices. It was more than we could afford.

So we dropped the main and jogged back and forth for an hour or so under jumbo and jib, looking at the island, so near yet so far away. I looked at the charts, looked at the sky, looked at the sea, felt the wind. It was a fresh easterly gale, but nothing extreme. It was dead downwind through the cut. I knew we could make it under sail. I called Bermuda Harbour Radio again.

"I'm having a hard time understanding why I can't sail in through the cut," I told him. "The wind's perfect for it."

"No problem, Cap. Come ahead."

The watch had changed and this operator was a sailor. So I called Lissa below and showed her our course on the chart.

"We leave the black buoys to starboard, the exact opposite of home."

"Ok."

"This one is the one we're looking at now. I'll call them out as I pass them, and you keep me off the reefs."

"Ok."

I handed her a flashlight because dusk was near, and went up on deck. I took the helm and steered for the cut. With just the headsails, *Avenger* was slow to answer the helm and wallowing in the big following seas. Steering was a job. Marty could see the problem.

"Like to have the foresail?"

"Can't. Halyard's on deck."

"I could shinny up and reeve it back through the block."

"We're rolling too much, Marty."

"I'm sure I can do it."

"Promise me you'll stop if it's too hard."

Marty nodded and, with Al in tow, went to the foremast. He lashed the bitter end of the peak halyard around his waist, and hauled himself up to the spreaders, hand over hand. My heart was in my mouth and I had to force myself not to watch so that I could keep her on course and under control. He stood in the spreaders, rove the halyard through the block and sent it down to Al, who grabbed it and held on for dear life. He wasn't letting it go a second time. Then Marty slid down the mast, I freed the foresail sheet and they raised the sail. As soon as it filled, things got better. *Avenger* got some speed and I got some control. We were booming along in the falling dark, apparently bound for a rock wall.

As we passed each buoy, Lissa verified it on the chart. I told her I still couldn't see the cut and there was a very nasty looking rock wall in front of us. She looked at the chart hard.

"It'll open up soon."

"Jesus. I hope you're . . . there. There it is."

Town Cut must be one of the most thrilling landfalls in the world. We came in off the wide ocean, surfing down a ten-foot sea into a narrow cut in the rocks and then, instantly, still water, the scent of flowers, the song of the peepers. Peace. It was dark as we sailed past the St. George's Dinghy Club. We couldn't see much. We found a place to drop the hook, furled the sails and hugged and hugged one another. We'd just done a fine piece of deep water sailing and we were tired and proud and happy.

I made a huge pot of stew and while it simmered, we drank a bottle of rum and laughed and talked til sleep fell on us like a Nova Scotia fog.

Stew is always better on the second day.

18

Arnold was a big horse, a Morgan, and not much to look at til he had a rider aboard. Then he arched his neck, pulled it all together and looked like the champion he was. He was trained for dressage. As a boy, I'd done some western style riding, but this was a whole 'nother thing.

"Gather him in," said Mike, his handler. "If you give him the right messages, he'll never do the wrong thing."

I was getting a riding lesson. I'd landed a part in *Mary Silliman's War*, a movie about the American Revolution that required some skill on horseback. When asked by the director if I could ride, I'd answered, "Like the wind." I needed the work. I hadn't made a red cent since the accident. As soon as I got the job, I found out who was providing the horses and called him. I figured I'd get the jump on the job if I knew the horse and he knew me.

"You and me, Arnold," I said, after my five-hour lesson. Arnold gave me a baleful look.

When I went to the hospital that evening, I was stiff and sore from riding. My ribs ached. Lissa was propped up in bed and had a couple of visitors. She was bright and cheerful. I told her about Arnold and my sore bum and she found it all very funny.

"Maybe you could put a pillow in your pants. (laugh) No. That would make your ass look big. (laugh) Is anyone likely to see this movie? (big laugh)."

All of this delivered with deadly timing. They say the sense of humour is a very complicated part of the brain. It was this part of Lissa that gave me the most hope. Even during these times, when her memory was shattered, she'd have moments like this, where she'd hold the room in the palm of her hand.

I was concerned about taking the film job. It would mean I'd have to miss seeing Lissa for a day or two. After her visitors left, I sat with her and we talked about it.

"It'll just be a day here and there. I think most of the shooting is in the Annapolis Valley. I should be able to get here most nights."

"It's all right, Tom. You need to work. Someone will visit me."

"I'll set it up so you're not alone after supper."

She sat there for a while, thinking. You could tell right away when something was bothering her. She was incapable of duplicity.

"Tom . . . why haven't my Momma and Daddy come to see me?"

"You don't know?"

"Haven't they heard that I'm hurt?"

I'd been dreading this moment, hoping her memory would find the truth before I had to tell it. She looked at me, so innocent . . .

"Lissa, your parents are both gone."

"You mean . . . "

Tears welled up, she writhed, the pain too much to hold. She was hearing this for the first time. Both of her parents were dead. She held her face in her hands, beyond comfort. Great sobs racked her. I got in bed next to her and held her as she wept. A nurse stuck her head in the room. I waved her off.

Lissa cried her heart out. I held her til she fell asleep. Then, I carefully extracted myself from the bed and tucked her in.

I found the night nurse and told her what had happened. I wanted her to know that if Lissa woke in the night and remembered what I had told her, she would be grieving and need comforting. Then I walked down the hill to the wharf where *Avenger* tugged at her lines.

Once aboard, I lit a fire and the lamp, and poured myself a rum. My journal was open on the table. I sat, took pen in hand, and stared at the blank page. I sipped the rum, stared at the page. I began to cry. I put the top back on the pen, laid it aside. I was holding it in, trying to get control of myself. I stood up, glass in hand and stared out the cabin window at the harbour. There was no one around. I drained the glass, poured another, breathing steadily, blinking back tears. I looked around the empty boat. My body was one huge ache and I could see no comfort anywhere. Standing was painful. Sitting was painful. I fell to my knees, then just crumpled there on the cabin floor.

"Help me . . . help me . . . "

I was losing it. I rolled over on my back and looked at the cabin overhead. It's mahogany tongue and groove with lighter ash deck beams. About dead centre there's an abrasion about an inch and a half long, left when the engine hatch in the cabin floor hit the overhead in the knockdowns off Newfoundland. I'd left it there to remind me how wild things can get, and as an effective bit of show and tell. As I snuffled back the grief, my eyes fell on the mark. It struck me funny. I smiled.

"Story of your life. One storm after another."

I stood up, poured myself a drink, drank.

"Interrupted by long, foolish bouts of fun and frolic, story and song, tender mercies and savage ecstasy, and voyages to the edge of . . . the edge of . . . "

I was feeling good again. Sad and lonely and good.

We were all up early, eager to get a look at Bermuda in daylight. St. George's is impossibly pretty. Pink, white and yellow buildings climbing up the hill around a harbour whose water is clear and turquoise. Rich vegetation, palm trees, flowers, and boats from everywhere. More than a few were showing evidence of damage from the storm we'd just sailed through. We made coffee and tidied up down below. I wanted things to look like we'd not even noticed the storm. Then we looked at the situation. The customs dock was on the inside end of Ordinance Island, and beyond it a narrow saltwater cul de sac created by a stone bridge. It was a tight fit without a lot of room to turn. We had no engine. We'd have to sail in.

We gave her the reefed main, fore and jumbo, hauled up the anchor and sailed down the harbour, then worked our way back up to the island. As we did, we talked about how to get her to the dock. The way the wind was blowing, still mostly east with a little south in it, we had to get sail off before we reached the dock and drift her up to it. It was a matter of not getting sail off too soon. We'd need enough way on to make it to the dock. If we didn't, we'd be in close quarters with nowhere to go and no way to get there. If we were going too fast, we'd bump into something unforgiving. You don't do things like this without crew like Lissa and Marty.

Once we'd all agreed what was going to happen, we made our approach. First the jumbo came down. Then the main. With just the fore, I made the turn which took us from close hauled to a reach. We picked up speed, dropped the fore and I turned for the dock. Perfect. Stone perfect. The customs lads were impressed. We were cleared with alacrity and good humour. And they let us lie to the dock for long enough to get a battery charged to start the engine, which was helpful since sailing out of there with the prevailing wind was not a possibility. We'd have had to row out an anchor and kedge her off.

We got the engine going, anchored near a derelict square-rigger and it was shore leave for all. We had friends in the anchorage. Corky and *Buccaneer Prince* got in a few hours before us. There were a couple of other boats that we'd met during *White Sails and Tall Tales*. We were excited and wide-eyed. This was our first foreign landfall.

Bermuda – proper, expensive, British to the bone – is also a place built on wreckers and pirates and tax evasion. The wreckers built fires along the shore to lure unsuspecting ships onto the reefs and pillage them. The pirates were free men, bearing letters from some king or other that allowed them to loot for the establishment, as long as the monarch profited as well. Some were good men, some were savages. The tax evaders are the embodiment of evil. Rich beyond imagining, they begrudge the nations that have made them rich a fair portion of their spoils, money that would provide that poor children could go to school, the sick to the hospital, and the weak could be protected. The pirates are small time now. The wreckers are gone. The tax evaders thrive.

We'd arrived on the island with five Canadian dollars. Not enough for a round of "dark and stormy's" at the White Horse. Lissa went into high gear. She told us to go to the White Horse and order a round and went to the little pink bank across the lane. Ten minutes later, she walked into the bar, all blond and beautiful and suggested that we should get a table by the water and order lunch.

We sat by the water, waiting for our cheeseburgers and chips (surely the universal "first meal" of offshore voyagers when they get ashore), and watched as tiny birds called sugar quince landed on our table and looked at us as if to say, "Where's the grub?" We remembered the passage with much laughter as we waited for our food. The newly wed and nearly dead were filtering in from various cruise ships and package tours, an alarming number in matching outfits, and filling the other tables.

We inhaled our burgers, Lissa paid the bill and we were off to explore the island. Marty and Davey went one way, Al another, and Lissa and I rambled through the tiny perfect town. First we found all the necessary places – the post office, the drug store, the grocery store, the laundromat. And we window-shopped, stopping into the exclusive boutiques whenever something caught Lissa's fancy. These places made me nervous but Lissa was fearless, no matter how proper the salesperson. I always figure they'll be mad if you don't buy something. Lissa had no such concerns. She'd look, ask questions, have them fawning over her and then say a cheery thanks and sashay out of there with me in furtive tow.

"No bargains in Bermuda, except maybe the woolens."

"We're bound south. We don't need woolens."

"You're a pitiful shopper, Tom."

"You're absolutely right. Let's find the sail loft."

In an ancient building along the waterfront, we found Ocean Sails and Steve and Jenny Hollis. They were sailors who lived on a twenty-eight-foot Paul-Johnson-designed-and-built double ender called *Little Venus*. Steve was Bermudan, Jenny from the States. Word was Steve could help with anything. He could. He looked you right in the eye, and in his quiet way made Bermuda feel like safe harbour. When we left the loft, Lissa gave my arm a squeeze.

"He's a keeper."

"No kidding. I'm starting to love this place even if it is too polite."

"Let's go that way."

We ambled along the shoreline til we came to Town Cut. As we stood there, amazed that just hours before we'd sailed through it in the dark, we saw a sailboat, bound in from the sea. We snuggled on a rock wall and watched.

"Bet they're excited."

"Strange looking boat."

"Look, Tom. She's from Canada."

She was a dark green double ender with a ragtag gaff rig and a tattered Canadian flag flying from the masthead. As she came through the cut we could see her three crew, bearded and clad in heavy wool sweaters and big black fisherman's rubber boots, leaping for joy. She was no gold plater.

"What kind of boat is that?"

"Hard to believe. It's a Gaspésienne. There were a bunch of them made after the war to fish from the Gaspé Peninsula. They had a reputation for being good sea boats. She's got to be fifty years old if she's a day."

"Do you know every boat in the world?"

"Nope. But I grew up on the North Shore. Before I had a boat I gave some thought to buying one. They were going cheap."

"I'm glad you decided on *Avenger*."

"Me too. But you have to love those guys for making it in that old hooker."

We continued our walk, following the coastline. It led us past beaches, an old fort, and then up over a hill through a golf course and back into St. George's. We came upon a magnificent ruin, an old church without a roof or windows. Turns out, it never had either, having never been finished. We couldn't resist the place. Once inside its stone walls, we noticed that we were alone, not a common thing on a fully crewed schooner. Lissa got that look in her eye, and we found a quiet corner. If God was watching, I'm sure She didn't mind. Afterwards, hand in hand, we ambled down the hill towards the harbour.

"Lissa, how'd you come up with the money for lunch?"

"Credit card. There's no more."

I never knew the truth about Lissa's wealth, and she never told me, except in the vaguest terms. But when things were rough, she was always there. She'd wait til all other avenues had been exhausted, then come to the rescue with just enough to squeak us through. Prudent management is what it was.

"Marty and I will make some money."

"How?"

"We could take our guitars to the White Horse, do some busking."

"I'll pass the hat."

"Done."

When Lissa passed the hat, our take doubled. She was hard to resist. We worked the White Horse and the Tavern on the Square and Marty sang in a church somewhere inland and soon had walking around money. We didn't eat out much, which is wise in Bermuda where the only superlatives regarding restaurants are the prices. We'd do dinner aboard before rowing ashore for a little socializing.

Hallowe'en was great fun. We had a couple of pumpkins aboard and Davey directed us in the making of jack-o-lanterns. There was to be a party on *Regina Maris*, so we got Davey dressed up as a pirate and with Marty and I as pumpkin bearers, Lissa and Davey went trick or treating through the quiet streets of St. George's. The jack-o-lanterns were a huge hit. Most folks had never seen a real one. Davey made a good haul.

The crew of the *Regina Maris* were as scurvy a lot of bloodthirsty pirates as you've ever seen. Davey's eyes got wider and wider as we climbed the gangplank of the ancient ship. The night was dark. The rig was hung with kerosene lamps. When the Chief Engineer hove into sight, he scared us to death. He was big and mean-looking and brandishing a wicked-looking cutlass. Before the night was over, he and Davey were mates, creeping around the ship striking fear in the unsuspecting revellers.

It was a merry crew that rowed back to *Avenger* that night. The candles in the pumpkins had burned out, and Davey insisted that they be recharged and lit and put out on deck, to keep us safe.

Down below, we drank and sang and Davey fell asleep wrapped in Lissa's arms.

19

THERE WAS A CARD SHOP between the boat and the hospital. I stopped in and bought a funny card for each day that I was to be working on the film. I wrote a note on each card reminding Lissa that I was being "Mr. Higgins" in a movie with a horse named Arnold and that I would be in to see her as soon as the work was done. I gave them to the nurses and asked them to give her one card each morning. I also made sure that our friends knew I might not be able to get in to see her so that they could take up the slack.

Most nights I got in to see her after the day's work. She liked to hear about my adventures aboard Arnold. Often, she'd have forgotten about the card and be worried about why I wasn't there, but she never forgot about the horse. I put a couple of the cards on the wall by her bed so she wouldn't forget. There was a sweetness about her that was heartbreaking. Some nights she'd ask about her parents and we'd have to go through the grieving again. Some nights she'd remember who'd visited her, and have a funny story.

There was one scene in the film that was to be shot in Shelburne, which was a four-hour drive from Halifax, while the scenes made in the Annapolis Valley were just an hour away. This meant I had to overnight there in order to be on the set first thing in the morning. I couldn't be sure that I'd get back to Halifax to see her the following day. She was getting worried that I was tired of her and drifting away. So I bought a teddy bear. I introduced Lissa to Bert the Bear, before leaving for Shelburne.

"Lissa, this is Bert. He's a friend of mine, and will remind you that I'll be back whenever you think I won't."

She took Bert in her arms, hugged and kissed him.

"Does Bert know how hurt I am?"

"Bert's a very sensitive and intelligent bear."

"I hope he has a good sense of humour."

"Funniest bear I ever met."

"Bert, you're not going to like hospital food."

She hugged Bert, smiled at me, childlike.

"I've got to get going. I'll see you as soon as I'm finished."

"Wave goodbye, Bert." She waved Bert's furry paw.

It was a radiant fall day. As I drove down the South Shore the memory of Lissa hugging Bert the Bear tugged at me. It was a relief to be in the outside world and going to work, but nothing felt real. Everything seemed to be at one remove. I felt like I was in a bubble, separated from the rest of the world by this goddamned accident.

I stopped at a convenience store and got a sandwich, a bag of chips and a bottle of water. Then I drove down by the water and pulled over, sat on a rock and dined alfresco. The place reminded me of the shoreline behind Lissa's old schoolhouse. I remembered her leading me through the woods to the shore and then leaping from rock to rock just out of reach of the surf. I remembered her boundless enthusiasm for the day. I remembered making love in a grotto in the rocks. She was everything a man could want. How had we come apart, and what would we now become?

She was getting better, but I was beginning to understand the depth of the injury. I still held to the dream of her complete recovery, or something close to it. But something was happening that I didn't bargain for. The Lissa I knew was slipping away. I had my memories, some good, some bad, but they were fading before the new person who was building herself right before my eyes.

When I arrived in Shelburne, I checked in to the bed and breakfast that the film company had booked for me, then walked to a pub I knew down by the water. I ordered a beer and some fish cakes, and was eating them when some of the cast and crew came in, full of laughter and high spirits. They gathered at a big table and ordered a round. They hadn't noticed me and I was thankful. I'd been looking forward to some socializing on the drive down, but now I just wanted to sit there and look out at the water. When the waitress cleared my plate, I ordered a double rum and another beer to chase it.

There's none happier than actors with a job. Most of the principals were at the big table, along with some production folks. They were an animated bunch. If armies could muster the kind of *esprit de corps* and "can do" attitude that is common with film crews, they'd never lose a war. It takes no more than a couple of days for a group of strangers to fuse into an efficient machine. It ain't always so, but this was a good shoot with a fine young director so the table was happy. I was sitting there enjoying their exuberance and sipping my rum when one of them noticed me and asked me to join the group.

I did. But I was out of place. My concerns were elsewhere and after some pleasantries, I excused myself and took the long way back to the B and B. Shelburne is a lovely old town. I ambled along, up one street, down another, carrying a moderate buzz. When the lights were on and the curtains open, I looked, and passed judgement on the decor. I'd give them a quiet "way to go" or "you can't be serious." Most were just friggin' lovely, with soft yellow walls, polite watercolours or oils, lots of antiques. Once, there was evidence of the dreaded fake wood paneling and velvet Elvis syndrome, but I was in the good part of town, so that was the exception. I almost knocked on their door and invited myself in. You have to figure they'd be fun. Folks with a velvet Elvis on the wall will always pour you a drink.

Back at the B and B, I was met by my kind innkeeper, who offered me a drink. We sat in the kitchen and talked. He was from Toronto and had retired here. He was just learning the place and still not quite "home." He loved the inn, and the town, but was gay, and while he felt little overt homophobia, he missed the extended family of the vibrant gay community he was used to. He wanted my story, and I was reluctant, but he persisted in his gentle way. So I told him. It took a while.

"She's lucky to have you."

"I think anyone would have reacted as I did. I've seen all kinds of heroism at the hospital."

"Perhaps so. But I'm no stranger to tragedy. I've seen it both ways. Some stay. Some go. You stayed."

"So far."

"You won't leave her. I know you won't."

He put his hand on mine, gave it a heartfelt squeeze. Then he told me about a dear friend who'd died of Aids and how it was to come to terms with all the changes.

"He was wicked, bold, fearless. Outrageous. Then he was diagnosed. At first he became even more vivid. Then his body started to fail him. He grew fearful. It was like it wasn't him anymore . . . and yet it was. That's when friends started falling away. They wanted him to stay the same, but he couldn't. And yet . . . it was still him . . . somehow . . . it was still him, perhaps more of him than any of us had ever seen."

Empathy. Why does it come naturally to some and seem a vacancy in others? What causes it to break down? If you look hard at the neo-con agenda that holds such sway nowadays, the vain trumpetings of the "Calgary School" in Canada and the Bush bunch in America, you can't help noticing that it's a philosophy that equates empathy with weakness. They talk about how a giving state weakens the population. They mean, of course, the recipients of the kindness. They contend that welfare kills incentive, makes people lazy. They seem unaware of the gifts conferred to those that do the giving. My circumstances made me hypersensitive to the absence of empathy in others. Every day I'd hear things that struck me as cruel and unfeeling. But now I was in the presence of a kind heart that understood my grief, and I took great comfort there.

We sat in the kitchen and sipped our single malt. He heard my lines, pronounced me ready for the camera. I admired his fine collection of iron skillets. We discussed the proper care and feeding of same.

❧

I STOOD AT THE GALLEY SINK, making coffee, looking out at the clear Bermuda morning. The harbour was alive with schools of fish feeding, sometimes leaping clear of the water. Melissa was stirring in our berth. The rest of the crew snored on. As the coffee dripped, I went over what needed to be done before we sailed on to the Caribbean.

"Captain Tom! Captain Tom!"

It was Davey's voice, calling from on deck. I was in the cockpit in a flash. Where was he? Maybe he'd fallen overboard.

"Up here, Captain Tom. I made it!"

As Lissa arrived in the cockpit, full of concern, I looked aloft. There he was, standing in the foremast spreaders, bursting with pride. Climbing the masts, hand over hand, was a sort of rite of passage in those days. Everyone tried. Davey had been working on it for months.

"Way to go, Dave!"

"You be careful up there!"

Lissa had never been too sure about allowing Dave to climb the rigging. Marty and I had argued that we'd make him clumsy and fearful if we didn't let him try. So Lissa had made sure that we discussed the do's and don't's with Davey. There had been a couple of "mast climbing" seminars.

"I can see out through the cut!"

"Make him come down, Tom." This quietly so Davey wouldn't hear.

"Ok, Dave. Let's see your technique for coming down. Take it slow around the spreaders."

Davey sat in the spreaders, hugged the mast and lowered himself carefully. As he made his way down, I gave Lissa a squeeze.

"Don't let him see how nervous that made you."

"I won't. The little bugger."

"He's a born sailor."

When Davey arrived in the cockpit all proud and happy, Lissa gave him a hug and felt his biceps.

"You're growing up too fast."

"No I'm not. I'm still a little boy."

Lissa got a wicked look, and grabbed him and jumped over the side, with Davey in her arms. They surfaced together, sputtering and laughing. When we'd arrived in Bermuda, Davey was a little shy about the water. He wasn't anymore. He was learning how to swim under Lissa's careful eye and the two of them did a couple of laps around the boat while I got towels and put them on the cabin roof and started breakfast.

I heard them laughing on deck as they dried off, wrapped themselves in towels and hung their wet clothes on the life lines. Lissa was perfect with Dave. When he needed a mother, she was a mother. When he needed a girlfriend, she was there. It was a hoot to listen to them flirt. They were besotted with one another. The rest of the crew was stirring, and breakfast was a lively affair, with Davey recounting in detail his journey up the mast.

Mike Pransche and Town Cut.

We added a crew member in Bermuda. Mike Pransche was an experienced schoonerman from Nova Scotia and an expert navigator. He was like a large troll crossed with a Viking, with blond hair, a big full beard and a ready laugh. I was glad to have him, and would learn a lot of shortcuts for working out sights from him on the passage. The "weather window" is much less critical for the trip south from Bermuda. You just make sure there's no late season hurricanes on the horizon and go. So, on the fourteenth of November, *Buccaneer Prince* and *Avenger* sailed out through Town Cut and shaped a course for St. Barth's.

The passage started in light winds and we squeaked out as much east as we could. Then it breezed up and we got her on the rhumb line going like a train. It was warm. We took deck showers, dipping up buckets of warm tropical water, dumping them over our heads, and sudsing up with Joy dishwashing soap. Mike and I took three sun sights a day, advanced our lines of position and compared the results. We knew where we were. I wrote a song once . . .

See there the Big Dipper,
And there the North Star.
At sea if you find them,
You know where you are.
But clouds they can hide them
And leave you for lost.
The secrets of heaven
Are won at a cost.

Navigation by the compass, the sextant, the sun and the stars is a bewitching art, one that confers the rarest and truest kind of liberty on the voyager. No juice is necessary. The satellites that inform the GPS can fall from the sky. The batteries can go dead. You can still look at the heavens and find yourself. The wisdom Mike passed on to me on that passage was well shared and treasured to this day.

As Mike and I lost ourselves in the sun and stars, the whole crew fell into the simple pleasures of a passage on the deep ocean. Watches came and went, meals were talked about, agreed upon and constructed to the delight of all. Melissa sailed past her seasickness and into the sea, tanned and fit and confident about herself and the boat. She and Davey dumped buckets of water on one another and their laughter ran through the boat like a rogue wave. We were a happy crew.

Lissa came on watch as I came off. We shared an hour, as we exchanged control of the vessel. I went to our berth, laid my hand on her shoulder. "Lissa . . . your watch."

"Mffff. Right. I'm awake."

I put the kettle on and brought the log book up to date. She dressed in the berth, climbed out and went to the head. By now all we were wearing was shorts and t-shirts, and if it was squally, a foul weather jacket. I finished with the log as she arrived in the galley and took over the coffee detail. We hugged. A big deep hug. I went on deck and made sure all was well. She filled the thermos with coffee, then poured two mugs and came on deck.

"Still sailing herself?"

"Like a train."

"I love this boat."

"I love you."

"Me to you, but it's a good thing you have such a great boat."

"Tell me something I don't know."

She found her place in the cockpit, settled in. I watched her, the way she looked at the sky, sniffed the wind, felt the schooner working her way through the sea.

"I didn't choose this, you know," I said.

"What?"

"Schooners. I never had a chance with schooners. I saw one sailing down the LaHave River when I was six. That was it."

"At least you've got reasons. What I'd like to know is, what's a hillbilly from Tennessee doing on a gaff rigged schooner in the middle of the ocean?"

"Why are your concerns always so much more interesting than mine?"

"Suck it up, Tom. You've met your match."

I knew that already.

Lissa and Dave.

20

MY SCENE WAS FINISHED BY NOON. I had lunch with the cast and crew at the Legion Hall and borrowed an assistant director's cellphone to call Lissa and tell her I'd be there after supper.

Her voice on the phone was tentative, a little afraid.

"Hello?"

"Hi Lissa, it's Tom."

"Oh . . . oh . . . I thought . . . I . . . "

She was crying. I waited til she settled down.

"I'm finished my scene so I'll be able to get there this evening."

"But . . . you had to go away."

"Just to Shelburne. It's a four-hour drive."

"Have I ever been to Shelburne?"

"We sailed there with *White Sails*."

"I . . . I'm no good, Tom. I can't remember."

"How's Bert?"

She brightened up immediately.

"He thinks he's the boss around here. He tells the nurses what to do."

"Funny. I never noticed Bert's pushy side. I'll see you tonight."

"You don't have to come."

"I want to. Give Bert a pill. Bye."

I was in the auditorium of the Legion Hall, where I'd gone seeking privacy and silence. A big empty room, with a stage at one end and stacks of chairs against the walls. I could hear the hubbub from the lunch room. It wasn't just Lissa who was changed by the accident. I love film work, the whole goofy brouhaha. I knew a lot of the cast and crew, and liked them all. Before the wreck, I'd have been in the middle of it, laughing and telling yarns. Now here I was, in an empty dance hall, wondering if there was a way to get out of there without having to talk to anyone.

When I got to the hospital, Lissa and Bert were ready for me. She'd enlisted the nurses and got her hair brushed and makeup done. Bert had a bow around his neck. He looked pleased with himself.

"Lissa, Bert, you both look just lovely."

"Bert made me get made up."

"You look beautiful, Lissa."

"Really? My hair . . . "

"I mean it. Beautiful."

She did. She'd held it in her mind that I was coming and prepared herself. There was more of her there. She was in command of herself. I told her about my turn before the cameras, and the kindness of the innkeeper. She listened with wide eye and sympathy. She had lots to talk about.

"Tom, did we ever live in Rose Bay?"

"No. We looked at a couple of houses in Rose Bay. We liked one, but you decided that the neighbours were too close by."

"A house on the beach?"

"That's the one we liked. It needed a lot of work."

"I wish my brain would straighten itself out. I was sure we lived in that house."

"Was it nice?"

"I can't remember."

We laughed. So did Bert, even though he didn't know why it was funny. This was the beginning of the "Rose Bay Fallacy," a persistent false memory that required months of gentle persuasion to delete from Lissa's shattered memory. Every time it came back it was more elaborate and Lissa clung to it with more tenacity. Part of the "fallacy" was that my name wasn't Tom. I can't remember what it was, and this may be a blessing.

We had a nice visit, joking about Bert and talking about this or that shard of memory. I was very tired and at some point, fell asleep in the chair beside Lissa's bed. I don't know how long I slept. Our friend Arthur dropped in and I woke up for his visit, then fell back to sleep after he left. It was one of those sleeps where you're still aware of your surroundings, drifting in and out of consciousness. Finally I forced myself awake. I looked at Lissa. She was holding Bert and looking thoughtful.

"I've been lying here trying to figure out who I am."

How many hale and hearty folks have no answer for that question? When you compare the futile confusion of all those people, the fortunes squandered in this or that therapy, to the urgent quest that Lissa was describing, a certain clarity is conferred. We are who we are, and given health, should live in gratitude. I didn't know what to say to her.

"You're my hero, Lissa, and have many admirers, including Bert."

"Was I a nice person before the accident?"

"You were a brave and loyal friend."

"But was I nice?"

"Yes you were. You made pies for the neighbours when you knew they weren't feeling well."

"I did?"

"Yes. Apple pies, peach pies, buttermilk pies."

"Tell me about our neighbours . . . "

And so it went. We talked for a while longer with me giving her thumbnail sketches of our neighbours and her struggling to remember them. Every now and then, a faint memory would come to light and she would be happy. It was getting late and visiting hours were over, so I kissed Lissa and Bert, and left the dark hospital.

As I walked down the hall, I could hear coughs and moans, cries of pain, and some rooms were quiet as the grave.

THE CLOSER WE GOT TO THE CARIBBEAN, the more squalls there were around. After you've sailed through a few dozen line squalls, you develop an ambivalent relationship with them. They're strange creatures. You see them in the distance, huge anvil-shaped clouds with a dark line between them and the water. The darkness is rain – rain like you've never seen, rain that falls so hard that it flattens the sea. Also in the cloud is wind, lots of it. Some squalls have sixty knots in them, though most are more like thirty. But they pass quickly, and the rain means fresh water for showers and drinking, and the wind means exhilarating sailing for a half hour or so. You have to be careful around squalls, but they can be fun. Usually, I try to avoid them, but not always, and sometimes you just can't get out of their way.

We were flying along in a big squall, with Al, Mike, Marty and Dave naked on the foredeck having fresh water showers. Lissa was steering. We'd cracked *Avenger* off to a broad reach so the bathers would have a gentler ride.

"Want a shower, Lissa?"

"Yes."

"Go for it."

I took the helm and she dashed below, got her shampoo and emollients, and reappeared in the cockpit, naked. She sudsed up, here, there and everywhere so to speak. It was an edifying spectacle. She had a wonderful body, and was free of neurosis about being naked when it made sense to be naked. I can still see her standing there, face to the wind, the rain coursing down over her, washing away the suds, and her glistening. Rinsed clean, she looked at me, smiled a wicked smile, did a little hoochey koochey dance and scampered below. I was a happy cappy.

The squall petered out, and I snugged up the sheets and called for the bathers on the foredeck to raise the foresail. Once back on course, all gathered in the cockpit for the cocktail hour. An ironclad tradition that has served the vessel and her various crews well, it involves everyone gathering an hour or so before sunset and sharing a rum and grapefruit juice. A cocktail known to all as the "Dumb Rum." The result is a release of tension, an explosion of humour, disclosure of anything peculiar about the boat.

"Cap, I thought I heard something fall on the deck last night."

"What?"

"Maybe a screw or something."

"And when were you planning on telling me?"

And so on. The leavening of the distillation of the cane is crucial to the operation. There's a reason for the deep affection sailors have for rum, and it goes beyond the obvious virtues of occasional oblivion. Taken in moderation at sea, it is powerful medicine. We were a clean and fragrant crew, invigorated by the squall, mellowed by the rum. Hilarity abounded.

Mike was rhapsodizing about his fresh new self.

"No, really, you have to smell my beard."

We smelled his beard. It was a meadow of wildflowers. Lissa sniffed last and went all soft and stroked his whiskers.

"Too bad you weren't in the cockpit, Mike. Lissa took a shower in the altogether."

Mike looked at me, crestfallen.

"Did you see her . . . ?"

"Her breasts?"

Mike's eyes were imploring. I nodded. He bit his thumb, sobbed. Lissa winked at Davey, said, "Don't look, Davey."

And she lifted her t-shirt and gave Mike a mighty flash, both of 'em, right in his face. Al took a picture. Davey laughed himself exhausted, and all of us went along with him, there being no way to resist.

All in all, an excellent cocktail hour.

Sunrise was perfect and Mike and I were sure we'd see St. Barth's before noon. It was nice to have someone else to share the pressure. I scanned the horizon, looking for land. Mike checked and rechecked our navigation. The rest of the crew were full of advice and speculation, secure that we were in command of the situation. There was a note of irreverence that Mike and I found unsettling. We were, after all, The Navigators, holders of the secrets of the sun and the stars. Where, oh where, was the respect?

Marty was very funny. He wandered about, looking for a clean shirt, sure that we were bound for somewhere dangerous and not at all on the charts. He communicated this with sidelong glances and questioning looks at the chart, little sighs and long searching sweeps of the horizon. Lissa was organizing her shoregoing wardrobe, and making beach plans with Davey. Al was oblivious, awash in a private bliss.

Mike was at the helm. I was on the foredeck, watching the clouds. An island usually has a dense cluster of clouds over it, especially later in the day when the heat has pulled the moisture out of the land. These clouds don't move like the rest. There was a suspicious clump on the horizon. Mike saw it too. And then I saw it, a saw-toothed little island, well off to starboard.

"Land ho!"

Mike stood, saw the island, nodded with a satisfied smile. Marty stuck his head up, looked, shook his head sadly, disappeared below mumbling about his shirt. Lissa and Davey were on deck in a flash, and very excited to see the island, off in the distance.

We were holding our course, keeping St. Barth's well to starboard. This was Mike's call. He'd been there before. Lissa was anxious.

"Why can't we just sail straight for it?"

A dark cloud crossed Mike's fragrant beard.

"Because."

"Oh."

There was tension in the air. Marty appeared holding up a shirt.

"Is this the kind of thing they're wearing in Havana?"

"St. Barth's!" shouted Mike in mock fury.

"Oh," said Marty, crestfallen. "Gonna need a different shirt."

"Lissa?" said Davey. "Why can't Dad just go naked?"

"The world just isn't ready, Davey."

"St. Barth's is the real Down South, right?"

Al, who stood on the stern with his elbows on the boom gallows, his long dark hair streaming in the trade winds, looking as good as he ever looked in his life, a cosmic goof in full flower, beamed at Davey.

"That's what we see on the horizon, Dave. DOWN SOUTH!"

Landfalls, like lovemaking, mustn't peak too soon. There was a degree of ecstasy in the cockpit that was unhealthy, given the fact that we were still six hours out. Cooler heads prevailed, and Marty decided to table the shirt question and make breakfast. Al went on watch. Lissa crawled back in her berth. Mike returned to his book and I brought the log up to date. This left Al and Davey in the cockpit. Al steered. Davey sat and visited, a habit of his that all aboard welcomed. This is what I heard.

"Al?"

"Yeah, Dave?"

"Down South . . . are there really naked women?"

"Well, Dave, they're not all naked all the time, but, yeah, there's definitely naked women Down South."

"Al?"

"Yeah, Dave?"

"They like it when you're cute."

"Truer words were never spoken. One thing a naked woman likes for sure is cute."

"Al?"

"Yeah, Dave?"

"When we get Down South, I'll be cute. You be old."

And so it was.

When we arrived in St. Barth's, Dave was cute, Al was old, Mike was fragrant, Marty sported a lovely shirt, I was as good as it ever got, and Melissa was beautiful.

She was the brightest star in a perfect tropical sky.

21

MEMORY CANNOT BE OBJECTIVE, nor impartial nor complete. Unharmed, it is imperfect if it is understood as a record of what actually happened. Harmed, it is a desperate thing, casting about for some reliable fact upon which to begin rebuilding a sense of self. Lissa and I were engaged upon a task that was impossible. Her memory was devastated. Mine was mine, and subject to all the revisions and misapprehensions my ardent self had found necessary over the years. When she asked me to tell her what happened, she wanted me to tell her what had happened to her. I didn't know. I only knew what I thought had happened to me. But I tried. I revisited our life together time and again, challenging my perceptions, striving to enter her world, her life with me from her point of view. It was at times an exercise in self-immolation that left me ashamed and afraid.

"Tom, did I always love you?"

"Not always. Sometimes you got mad at me."

"But even if I was mad, I would still love you, wouldn't I?"

"I don't know, Lissa. I'm not you."

"Do you stop loving people when you're mad at them?"

"No."

"Then why do you think I would stop loving you?"

"I'm not saying that, Lissa. It's just that . . . I'm trying to let you be you."

"But I don't know what I was like. I don't remember. You must remember what I was like."

"You were brave and sexy and adventurous and smart and funny and loyal and . . . "

"There must have been some bad things."

"You were bossy."

"No I wasn't."

These were my devotions, these conversations, my masters, my meditations, my most brilliant teacher. What did she remember? Her parents. Her family. Marty, Davey, Cathy, Michael, Gethin, Cecily, Eric, Belinda, Chris, Wenda, Bill, Betty, Lenny, Susan, Arthur, David, Sandra, Corky, Lee, John, Peg, Willie, Doo Dah, Beltoe, Kasha, Carl. And more, so many more. I could fill pages with people. Always people. She may have forgotten the context, but she remembered every soul that had touched hers, and was accurate about the depth of the touching. People were the touchstones that gave Melissa Andrelle Groseclose her life. People were the foundation of her recovery. And her memory of them was entirely equal to the love she had for them. Is there a more eloquent argument for the value of friendship?

Lissa's occupational therapist would take her in a wheelchair to a special room to work with her. I was invited to one of their sessions. One wall of the room was a large mirror. Across from the mirror, there was a large padded platform. The O.T. got Lissa, unsteady as a newborn, out of the chair and onto the platform. Then she got on the platform with her, got her facing the mirror and propped her up in a sitting position.

"Look, Lissa. Can you straighten your shoulders?"

Lissa would look, try to adjust herself with the O.T. providing balance. For the O.T. this was physical work involving a lot of intimate contact. She was very tender with her. Every little advance was remarked upon. She was trying to make Lissa aware of her body, reconnect the circuits that had been severed by the injury. I was daunted by the magnitude of the task.

It wasn't easy to see how any of this could work. Lissa was like a rag doll and struggled with every move. But after a while, a pattern began to emerge, and you could see that Lissa was becoming more aware of the demands the activity was making on her. Then the O.T. let go of her and she fell over.

"Sit up, Lissa."

I wanted to intervene, to tell her that this was too difficult.

"Look in the mirror."

Lissa did.

"I look awful."

"See. Your left arm isn't doing anything."

Lissa went to work. She lined her arms up to best advantage for the job. This took a few minutes of struggle.

"I can't."

"Roll over on your side . . . that's it. Now push yourself up."

She tried one way, then another. Finally, she got a little advantage and got herself about halfway vertical. Then, she was stuck. She couldn't figure out which hand to use next.

"Look in the mirror, Lissa. See your left hand? It isn't doing anything."

Lissa looked, moved the hand, lost her balance and fell back. She was on the verge of tears. The O.T. looked at the situation, tried again.

"Shall I help you?"

"No! I have to be able to sit up."

This time, she rolled onto one side, looked at the mirror, got her hands positioned, mustered all her strength and sat upright. Then she looked at the mirror and began to capsize. The O.T. steadied her, then took her hand away.

"You did it, Lissa. I didn't help."

Lissa still didn't look right. The O.T. got behind her and wrapped her arms around her shoulders. With both of them looking at the mirror, she adjusted Lissa's posture til she was lined up in a more natural position. Then she let go, and Lissa sat there looking at herself.

"Is my eye opening?"

We all looked. It was. Her left eye was about half open.

"Can you see out of it?"

Lissa closed her right eye, then opened her left eye a little more with her finger.

"It's blurry, but I can see."

"Good. It'll come back."

As we wheeled Lissa back to her room, we were a cheerful bunch. Lissa kept closing her right eye and holding the left one open, looking around her trying to make the eye work better.

Ever so slowly, Lissa was working at taking command of herself. One day she pulled her catheter out in a fit of pique. It was uncomfortable and she didn't like it. This added a new dimension to my visits. We'd be chatting away, making our way from person to context to story, and she'd get a concerned look.

"Tom . . . I have to tee tee."

I'd leap into action. They had a couple of mobile commode chairs on the ward. I'd find one, wheel it into the room, and park it beside the bed. Then we'd get her sitting up with her legs dangling over the side of the bed. I'd hoist her to her feet, pull her pants down and place her, as gently as possible, on the convenience. She'd do her business. I'd get some toilet paper from the bathroom, she'd wipe, and I'd help her stand.

We'd get her shorts up, hoist her back up onto the bed and I'd empty and rinse the bucket and park the thing outside our door. We got very good at this over time, and there were few mistakes. When they did happen, they were the cause of profound grief, sometimes fury.

All I could do was stand amazed as she fought for a life she couldn't be sure was worth the struggle.

IN THOSE DAYS, ST. BARTH'S was still a quiet little island, just beginning to be discovered by the rich and famous. The gathering place for sailors was Le Select, a great little bar in an old colonial building made of stone. It was on a corner and had a fenced-in garden, with shells underfoot and big bougainvillea trees overhead. The tables were mismatched, the bar room itself a riot of pictures, posters and sailing burgees. The cocktail of choice was the lethal "ti punch," which consisted of two ounces of rum, half an ounce of cane syrup and a squeeze of lime. A couple of those and you entertained thoughts of immortality.

Once again, *Buccaneer Prince* had beaten us in by a day, and Corky had primed Marius, the beloved owner of Le Select, for Marty and me. He'd told him we were well-known professional musicians from Canada. So when we arrived, Marius asked if we'd like to play in the bar. No money would be involved, but drinks would be free. We already knew that Jimmy Buffett played there for free so were eager to offer our services. We figured the sooner we established our credentials on the island, the sooner we'd find a paying gig. We were booked for Saturday night.

November is a special month in the islands. The hurricane season is over and the tourist season about to begin. All is anticipation. Lissa and I explored the town of Gustavia, and revelled in the rich mixture of French, Creole and West Indian cultures on offer. Both of us are drawn to places where "real life" is going on and are put off by places that are obviously set up to fleece the tourists. St. Barth's was on the cusp, but the locals still held sway. Raggedy old island trading sloops unloaded cargoes of fruit and loaded with wine and spirits for down island at the town dock. Eccentric local shops with names like "Smoke and Booze" sold all manner of things, from fabric to pots and pans, as well as the advertised commodities. Loulou's Marine was a good little chandlery run by a local sailor-entrepreneur named Loulou Magras, who had a wry sense of humour and a welcoming smile.

At four each afternoon we'd go to Le Select and find the rest of our crew there, as well as an international cast of characters who provided an ongoing narrative that was never less than interesting. Champagne Jim Green would come waltzing in, Max, the bartender, would see him, put Ringo Starr's version of "You're Sixteen, You're Beautiful and You're Mine" on the sound system, turn it up to melt and start opening the bubbly. A cluster of models from some European fashion shoot would catch his eye. At another table, Eric Taberlay, the great French racing sailor, and Paul Johnson, a world renowned sailboat designer/builder/sailor, discussed the perils of dry land.

By the Wednesday before Marty and I played, the island had been papered with homemade posters promising "Live Canadian Music." We wondered what the natives thought that might be. We were learning the etiquette of the place, the "kiss kiss" greeting, the hierarchy of the tables, the offering and accepting of drinks. Under Marius' gentle presence, Le Select was an invigorating mixture of politesse and anything goes. We soon found ourselves well provided with friends and fellow travellers.

By Saturday night, Marty and I were getting a little concerned about the level of excitement that was building about our performance. A sound system had been procured, and everyone was planning to be there. We even practiced a few tunes, to make sure we could remember what to do. We always worked "without a net," no set list, no fixed arrangements. Marty is a great guitar player with ears like an elephant. I'm a good rhythm player, but like to know the tune before I perform it. Both of us play harmonica, both of us sing harmony and lead. Marty knows a million songs. I'm at home with stuff I've written, and have a small selection of "covers." Our act was half original songs, half old songs that have stood the test of time.

With Lissa as wardrobe consultant and coach, we got ready for the show and rowed in to Le Select. The place was jammed to the rafters, and vibrating with excitement. I looked at Marty, he looked at me.

"S'pose there's something going on here tonight?" said Marty.

"Nothing that makes sense."

Lissa used her alchemy to secure a table inside, near the "stage" for her and Davey. Marty and I went out back, tuned up and after a set by a bunch of local outlaws called Willie Makit and the Contraband we plugged in and went to work. We had no idea what to expect, but were pretty sure we were overmatched. Two guys with accoustic guitars vs. a seething mob that spilled out onto the street. We were ready to settle for a draw.

The gods were kind. From the first note, the crowd was with us and we could do no wrong. Neither of us could believe the reaction, and spurred on by the approval, we spun out song after song to a sea of smiling faces. We both remember that night as one of the special ones. It's not often you sing to a room full of people from all over the world, from the rich and famous to the poor and obscure, and find them all in agreement. There were many encores, and we were an exhausted and happy pair when we sat down with Marius to drink the champagne he poured to celebrate the success of the evening. Lissa and Dave had made a hundred friends during the evening, and he slept with his head on her lap as we drank bottle after bottle of Moët with Marius and Fast Eddy, his son. Al was convinced that the entire building had levitated during the last set, and that Marty and I were destined to conquer the world.

Back aboard *Avenger*, we put Davey to bed and sat up finishing the two bottles of champagne Marius had pressed into our hands as we left.

"If there's one thing I like," said Lissa, as I filled our glasses again, "it's too much champagne."

22

THE VICTORIA GENERAL HOSPITAL, now the Queen Elizabeth II Health Sciences Centre for reasons known only to royalty-sensitive euphemism-happy bureaucrats, was and is a great hospital but, for all its charms, it was wearing thin. If there ever was an illustration of the inadvisability of top down design, it's hospitals. They don't have to be such depressing places. It wouldn't cost any more to make them welcoming, humane and beautiful. Talk to the patients. Talk to the nurses. Hell, hire the student body of an art college and turn them loose. Trust me, things would improve. Lissa and I struggled to make the best of things as they were. I'd take her to the Public Gardens to feed her ducks. Sometimes I'd wheel her down Spring Garden Road so she could window shop.

"Oh . . . oh. Is that me?"

"What?"

She was looking into a window, seeing her reflection.

"Take me home. Ah look like shit."

Her Southern accent was quite thick as she relearned how to talk.

"You don't look like shit. You look hurt."

"Hurt. He hasn't called, he hasn't written."

"The gorilla joke!"

"Did Ah just remember something?"

"Nurse gets kidnapped by a gorilla, and . . . "

"He has his way with her, over and over and over . . . " She struggled to remember the rest. I prompted her.

"After a few weeks of jungle debauchery she escapes."

"The hospital! She's in the hospital and her friend visits and says, 'Mah God, girl, they say you were raped by a gorilla. Are you hurt?'"

"And she says . . . "

"'Hurt? He hasn't called, he hasn't written . . .'"

You had to be there. You really did.

Thanksgiving was a big deal that fall. My sister Cathy's sister-in-law Allison lives in Halifax with her husband Walt and some large, bright sons. Cathy and Michael came to Halifax from Prince Edward Island, and a big family dinner was planned. This was to be Melissa's first "evening out." Wardrobe was discussed, fears and worries dealt with, excitement shared with the nurses.

I can't remember what we did about her hair. Half her head, exactly half, had been shaved bald. By now there must have been quite a stubble. I remember her first haircut happening later when the short side got long enough that the result would be a success, so she must have had a Picasso hairdo, though I don't remember it that way. I remember her looking wonderful. Now I don't mean to be knocking Picasso. He's a real good painter, but those hairdos. Maybe she wore a headband or scarf or something.

I wheeled her out of the hospital at around four in the afternoon on a fine fall day. We managed the transfer from wheelchair to car with ease. I drove the long way so she could look at the fall colours. When we arrived, strong hands were there to hoist Lissa and the chair up onto the porch and into the house. Inside, nothing but smiling faces. I'm sure little victories like this happen every day. Somehow, they must add to the fund of goodness in the world. I watched the family making a fuss over Lissa and her revelling in it.

A splendid table was set, and a feast laid before us. Among the most persistent worries had been management of the utensils. I'd been feeding her just weeks ago. Every physical act required conscious volition. She'd worked at it for days, at every meal. Not only did she manage all of it with aplomb, but she contributed mightily to the general well being.

"Matt, you're just too good lookin' to have these two for parents."

Matt's parents are, it must be said, a handsome couple.

Returning to the hospital that night was particularly melancholy. Lissa had loved being in the real world and by the time I wheeled her into her little room, she was crying. Together, we got her out of her clothes and into a t-shirt and shorts. Then she got into the bed, almost by herself. She was able to stand with something to steady herself. I noticed each little advance in physical prowess. When some little task seemed to make the transition from laboured and thoughtful to natural and easy, I counted it a victory.

Once she was in bed, and had Bert in her arms, I got in bed beside her and we snuggled and talked about the evening. She remembered some of it, and then there would be blanks, which upset her. We went over the whole thing, step by step, and I could tell when she was really remembering, and when she was pretending to make me feel better. This process, which was constant, was a serious test of my patience and forbearance. Simple things would slip away, others would stick in her memory and grow out of proportion to their importance. I had to maintain an even temperament concerning all of it. If I got frustrated, she could read it like a book and would close down, or get hurt and confused. Sometimes, she would be consumed by anger at herself or me or both of us. There seemed nowhere to turn for advice about any of this. But that was about to change.

"I'm never going to get better, am I?"

"How can you say that? We went out to dinner tonight and you were wonderful. You couldn't have done any of it a month ago."

"Really?"

"Ask Bert."

"Bert always agrees with you."

"Bert's a good bear. We're moving to the Rehabilitation Centre next week. They know lots about helping you to get better."

"I'm afraid, Tom."

"I would be too if I'd been hurt like you."

"Really?"

"You're very brave, Lissa."

"But I'm afraid."

"If you're not afraid, there's no need for courage."

I stayed with her til she fell asleep in my arms, then extracted myself from the bed and went back to the boat. It was cool down below, so I lit a fire and sat in my coat and waited for the heat to fill the cabin. It took a while. The rum helped.

❧

AL MOVED ASHORE AFTER A COUPLE OF WEEKS and took to guerilla camping on the beach and in the bushes. Mike found a ride to Antigua and got a job driving a Swan 47, a Swedish-built millionaire's sloop. That left Marty, Davey, Lissa and me, and would that every captain could have such a crew. Davey was the glue. We were all delighted by his enthusiasm. He was becoming a fine swimmer, could row as well as any of us and made friends like magic. Lissa would take him to the beach, and they'd come back with more kids in tow. The boat was teeming with life.

In later years I installed a shower and fridge, but things were basic in those days. There was ice to carry and bathing

was done in the sea, with a rinse from the shower bag that hung in the shrouds. Around four each afternoon, we'd all leap over the side with a bottle of Joy. We'd climb into the dinghy, suds up, and dive back in, swim til the soap was gone, then climb back aboard for the fresh water rinse. The whole operation involved much laughter and foolishness. Despite the luxury of the hot shower we now have down below, I miss this ritual.

Our poverty dictated eating aboard most of the time. Lissa and I shared the cooking, though she carried most of the load when we were at anchor. She's an adventurous and talented cook and was eager to use the local foods and methods. We'd buy plantains and christophenes from the Dominican women on the dock and she'd get into long conversations about what to do with them. She addressed them with wide eyes and an open heart and was met with the same. They taught us the difference between "seasonin' peppers" and "Scotch Bonnets," crucial knowledge if you value your palate. We learned to love pigeon peas and rice and fresh local fish. After dinner, we'd have "The Adventures."

I'd sold Davey on the proposition that, due to the metal in my fillings, I had a radio in my head. One ear was the on-off switch. The other, the tuner. He'd turn the ear, I'd make a click, he'd turn the other ear, I'd make the sound of a radio being tuned, with static and snatches of each station passed, until we arrived at the right station. Then it was – in a stentorian announcer's voice – "The Adventures of Gypsy Davey and the Schooner *Avenger* . . . brought to you by Rats Crapskies, the cereal that makes you get up in the morning, say 'Rats!' take a crap and go Skiiiiing!" And we'd all sing the jingle: "Snort, chortle, poop, Rats Crapskies."

The story would follow. The characters were Gypsy Davey, Gypsy Daddy, High Seas Lizzy and Cap'n Tom. There was enough of what was really happening to us each day in every episode that Dave willingly suspended disbelief for the parts about Black Jack Scabbard and his pirate ship that sailed in the clouds. And Mumbo Kajumbo and Black Magic Island. And Princess Viva who was his paramour. They were cliffhangers, always leaving the *Avenger* and her stalwart crew in dire straights at the end of each episode. "The Adventures" went on for years, whenever we were together, and Davey continued to pretend belief in the radio in my head long after it made any sense.

Were there hardships in those days? Yes. Money was short. It takes a toll, living in close quarters. Feelings would get hurt. People would need time alone. But the whole operation was fueled by deep affection and respect and a shared sense of humour. Marty was sensitive about giving Lissa and me time alone, and he and Davey would go off on rambles. Lissa and

I knew that it was difficult for Marty, being without a home of his own, and we made sure he knew how appreciated he was. And always, there was Davey. Nothing compares to the gift that is a happy child. When he got cranky, which wasn't often, we'd hurl him over the side and dive in after him. We'd surface together, laughing.

St. Barth's, for all its virtues, was proving a hard place to find paying gigs so we weighed anchor and sailed to Philipsburg in St. Maarten. Even then, it was getting too developed, but that meant there were lots of bars that needed music. We found a regular gig at a place called Pinochio's. Marty and I would sing, Lissa bartended and kept an eye on Davey, who became an expert at the Pacman game that sat in the corner. The bar itself was round with a tree growing up in the middle, and would take about a hundred people standing three deep. How Lissa remembered what everyone drank and kept the tabs straight is a mystery to me, but for as long as the gig lasted, we were in the money. Lissa's tips were the icing on the cake.

We were always hungry after work, so we'd hoist Davey, who'd be sleeping behind the stage, on our shoulders and go to El Gordos. This was a Volkswagen van that had been turned into a fast food joint. They served peas and rice and fried chicken and fish. And it was good. We'd get three plates and head down the dock to the dinghy, still carrying Davey. One of us had two guitars, one had Davey, one had the food. It was a nice piece of work getting all of it back to the boat without mishap. The thing is, by now Davey was awake but pretending to be asleep because he liked being carried. You had to be quick to catch him at it. We'd come up alongside the boat. I'd put the guitars on deck. Lissa would climb aboard with the food. I'd hold on for Marty and Davey. Marty would say something like, "Davey's dead to the world. Let's just leave him in the dinghy."

"No way!"

"Why not? You're asleep."

"Am not."

"Are too."

"Look. My eyes are open. I'm talking!"

"You could be sleep talking."

"Dad!"

We'd sit in the cockpit and eat our chicken, washing it down with Mount Gay and lime. Davey would pass out as soon as he'd wolfed down a leg, and pad off to his bunk. Lissa would tuck him in. Then she'd send me, and I'd send Marty. Dave would always thank us for the day. Back in the cockpit we'd freshen our drinks, and straighten out the universe. Often, we'd talk until dawn.

We worked two nights a week and soon tired of Philipsburg. The harbour was dirty and didn't invite swimming. There was too much traffic. We decided to sail to Anguilla for a change of scene on our days off. So we provisioned, raised the sails, weighed anchor and fell into the sweet tropical breeze.

By now, sailing the boat was second nature to all of us. Stowing for sea took ten minutes, and getting away another five. We were still getting used to the constancy of the trade winds. Sometimes they blow hard, twenty-five to thirty knots. Sometimes ten to fifteen. But you seldom have to wait for wind in the tropic winter. You raise the sails and you're booming along.

As we sailed down the length of St. Maarten, we could see the scars in the landscape that rampant development was making. Half the island is Dutch, St. Maarten, half French, St. Martin. Both sides were being built up at a ferocious rate. It was a laboratory for unfettered capitalism, and it wasn't pretty.

Aboard *Avenger*, Lissa sunbathed on the foredeck, Marty was at the helm, I lounged on the bowsprit, and Davey trolled for fish.

23

THE EXPEDITION TO THE Rehabilitation Centre was longed for but a bit of a wrench when it happened. My sister and niece came to help, and we rounded up carts for Lissa's things. There were clothes, luggage, teddy bears, vases of fresh flowers and all manner of memorabilia. There was a wooden folk art alligator that friend Tom from the Soho Restaurant had brought to defend her from the jumbies. There were pictures, a tape recorder and cassettes. It was a two-cart wagon train, with Lissa in the wheelchair – Bert the Bear in her arms – that finally made its way out of the ward after a round of hugs and tears.

The hospital and Rehab Centre are connected by a tunnel under the street. We rumbled along, with niece Cecily's merry laughter to calm Lissa's fears of the unknown. And mine. What was this place going to offer us, and what were they going to expect of Lissa?

I needn't have worried. We were met by Dr. Brenda Joyce, who knows more than most about head injuries. A pretty blond with sympathetic eyes and a straightforward manner, she inspired confidence and hope, while letting you know that the road ahead would not be easy.

The centre was a nicer looking place than the hospital. There was varnished wood overhead, good lighting, and big windows in the rooms that let in lots of light. Lissa had a roommate at first, and this took some adjustment after the private room in the hospital. After we moved in, Cathy and Cecily left us alone. Lissa's fears were near the surface, but she was fighting them down. Then a nurse's aid named Christa breezed into the room. She was heaven sent.

Christa and Lissa connected immediately. Lissa made a joke, Christa laughed, and they were off to the races. Christa told us what the days would be like, with physiotherapy, occupational therapy, speech therapy and so on. I was informed that I wouldn't be allowed to visit until four each afternoon.

"But he comes every morning." Lissa didn't like the sound of this.

"You'll be in the gym and the pool and too busy for visitors during the day. Besides, absence makes the heart grow fonder." Christa held Lissa's hand as she said this.

"But I'll forget who he is."

"That's handy. You won't get bored with him."

They let me stay til bedtime. I made a little note with a cartoonish self-portrait for Lissa that reminded her that I'd be there at four o'clock the next day and left her there, looking just a little lost.

I didn't know what to do with all the free time I'd just been granted. I went down to the boat and checked her lines, then decided to drive home and check on the house and the cats.

Little Bits was glad to see me. I built a fire in the fireplace and one in the kitchen stove and started going through the mountain of mail on the table, mostly bills and threatening documents from Revenue Canada. There was nothing but trouble. The tax thing was all out of proportion. They were doing a net worth audit and had concluded that we owed them hundreds of thousands of dollars. I wanted to show it all to those who knew how close to the bone we'd always lived.

You'd have to have made millions to owe that kind of money. They were basing their assumptions on the fact that we owned a beautiful sailboat and shore property.

Here's what happens. You find a beautiful boat, buy it with a mortgage for a small price because it's wood. Then you spend years working on her, making her more and more beautiful. You're living aboard as you do this, so your mortgage payment is your rent. You are not rich, but have a rich man's boat, or so it appears. Enter the bureaucrats. They have no category for folks like you, and they will not listen. You have a yacht, and no one with a yacht can live on what you're declaring according to the book, so you're a criminal. Period. Once they've made up their alleged minds, you're screwed. They've decided you're guilty. You must prove your innocence. But you're arguing with stuff that they've made up. And what happens to you depends upon who gets your file. There seems to be no set standard.

"Revenue Canada."

"Can I speak to Mr. Blivit? (Name changed to protect the guilty.)

"Hello, Blivit speaking."

"Hi. My name's Tom Gallant and you guys figure I owe you three hundred thousand dollars."

"Yes, Mr. Gallant."

"I don't owe you three hundred thousand dollars."

"We have documents that suggest otherwise."

"Suggest?"

"Well, we have to make certain assumptions, since you've been less than forthcoming."

"My wife did our taxes and she wouldn't lie about that stuff. She was too careful."

"Why don't you let me talk to her?"

"You did talk to her, the day you came here with the strange guy who wouldn't say anything, who my banker tells me was a cop."

"Your banker . . . ?"

"You guys went to see him after you saw us and the guy told the banker he was a cop and we were criminals."

"Oh."

"That's illegal, you know."

"It is? How do you know?"

"I asked a lawyer."

"Oh. Well, have your wife call me."

"We had a bad accident. My wife has a catastrophic head injury. She remembers none of this, and she has enough trouble now, just trying to learn to walk. You're talking to me, and I know this thing is wrong."

"You'll have to prove it."

And on and on and on. No one would explain how they'd arrived at the numbers they were quoting as gospel. No one would allow that our circumstances were worthy of being considered. No one would address the illegality of the presence of the Mountie in our kitchen. No one would tell me if there were charges being contemplated. Fact is, guilty or innocent, there's no hope once the dreaded Net Worth Audit is rolled into your driveway.

I looked at the pile of paper on the kitchen table and wished I was a thousand miles offshore, hove to in a mighty gale.

WE ROUNDED ANGUILLITA, a tiny island off the end of Anguilla, and hardened the sheets, bringing *Avenger* close to the wind. Anguilla is low and flat, and there's deep water in close, so you boom along in flat water with your sails full of warm wind. It's one of the best day sails in the world. Usually the islands are mountainous, and while the lee offers flat water, the winds are baffling. But not Anguilla. Anguilla is flat and the wind is perfect. We slipped along sipping cold Heineken, which was dirt cheap on Dutch St. Maarten, and plotted our free dinner at the Barrel Stay.

The Barrel Stay was a relatively new place at the time, stylish in a rustic West Indian way. It was right on the beach, open to the trade winds from the tin roof to the railings made mostly of barrel stays, with colourful chairs from Haiti and tables that were barrels with wooden tops. It was run by Bob from New York, and Jean and Marie Lou from Belgium. We had a standing invitation to bring our instruments and sing for our supper. The food there was beyond spectacular. We all had designs on the fantastic fish soup and something Creole to follow.

We sailed into Road Bay, picked a spot just off the beach close to our dinner destination and sailed her to the hook. Anguilla's national sport is sailboat racing. All along the beach, beautiful local racing sloops are pulled up under the palms. You make a lot of friends by sailing smartly into the place, especially if you're sailing a gaff rigged schooner. The locals knew *Avenger* was from Nova Scotia by looking at her. They'd had many old Lunenburg schooners in the glory years of sail, working out their declining years hauling fish, salt, rum, fruit, whatever they could find. Anchored in the bay near us was the Prime Minister's *Warspite*, a storied old Anguillan-built cargo schooner with a reputation for speed. I loved the place.

There's a thing about winter in the Caribbean that's always a surprise to the uninitiated. Since the weather feels like summer, you expect summer light. Not so. It's winter. The sun lasts exactly twelve hours. They turn it on at six, turn it off at six. Blam. Out go the lights. So we rowed ashore in the dark. Three adults, one child, two guitars in a little dinghy. Good thing we were used to this routine because there was a little surf rolling in. We landed on the beach without upset, dragged the dinghy up the beach, and walked into the Barrel Stay. There were two or three tables of tourists, who looked at us as if we were aliens, since we'd just materialized out of the dark.

Jean and Marie Lou met us with kisses and smiles and the gig was on. We were fed a beautiful meal, and then espresso and cognac. We took out our guitars, pushed our chairs back from the table and commenced to sing. Oh, it was lovely. By now Marty and I had our act down pat. Well, pat for us. We still worked without a net, but we had developed a connection that kept us safe and provided delight to us as well as the audience. After our first set, an elderly gent who had been dining with a younger woman came to us and asked if he could play violin with us. For some reason, our usual wariness about such offers didn't apply and we said sure and the young woman went to get his instrument.

The guy was great! He played like Stephan Grapelli, and the whole thing became a transcendent experience. Folks were dancing. Locals gathered under the palms outside the restaurant and listened. Jean couldn't contain himself and started opening champagne. Somehow, we found a long set of tunes that all of us could play together, and no one could believe that we were strangers. In a way, we weren't. After the set, as he put his fiddle back in the case, he shared a bit of his story.

"I used to play professionally when I was young, but had to give it up and take over the family business. Sold the business after my wife died. I don't know why I'm lucky enough to be with Rachel here, but she's the one who made me bring the fiddle. She's the one who made me play tonight. Haven't got the chops I used to have, but you fellas just added ten years to my life."

"Are you kidding? You play great. You did us a favour."

And we sat in a big circle and shared champagne and stories, and Jean and Marie Lou didn't want it to end. Nobody did.

It was a well-lubricated crew that launched the dinghy off the beach and rowed back to the *Avenger*. Davey pulled his sleep trick, and we had big fun passing him back and forth. A couple of times, he fought down giggles but we played along with him and passed him from one to the other til he was snug in his berth. Then we kissed him, Marty crawled in beside him, and Lissa and I retired to the cockpit.

"Too much champagne again. I'm sorry, Lissa."

"You better be."

"What about a walk on the beach?"

"What about it?"

We rowed ashore and walked. When there's a moon in Sandy Ground, the water is captured light on the beach. It's warm on your feet, weightless. We found the perfect spot. Then we made love. Afterwards . . .

"Tom, we can't live like this forever."

"Why?"

"What about when we're old? We won't be able to handle the boat. We'll have medical problems. It's fine now, but sooner or later, we're going to have to take care of bidness."

"Haw haw. Bidness. I'd rather die in a gale because I'm too old and weak to reef."

"I know you would. That's what worries me."

"Well, as long as that's the worst of your worries."

24

WHEN I GOT TO THE REHAB CENTRE, Lissa's room was empty. A nurse told me she was still in the gym and would be up soon. I waited in her room until an attendant rolled her in. She saw me, burst into tears. She was flushed and tired.

"Oh . . . oh . . . I thought you wouldn't come."

"I always come. What did you do today?"

"They wore my ass out."

She wheeled herself to the bed and parked beside it. Then she fussed with the chair til the arm next to the bed flopped down. She fussed with the chair some more, remembered, put the brake on. Then she transferred herself from the chair to the bed. It wasn't pretty, but she did it, ending up on her back, staring at the ceiling, her legs dangling over the side.

"That's what we did . . . I think."

"That's amazing."

"No. No. It's awful, Tom. I can't walk. I think Karen doesn't like me."

"Karen?"

"My physio. She never smiles. She was very strict."

I liked the sound of Karen. Lissa was far too good at charming people into letting her do what she wanted. She needed a tough coach.

"If she's working you hard, maybe that's because she wants you to get better."

"Help me."

She was struggling to get situated on the bed. I helped her get her legs up and then tried to hoist her up towards the head.

"No . . . no . . . the pillows! Fix the pillows!"

Her voice was angry, insistent.

"What do you want me to do with the pillows?"

She was losing her temper, thrashing around. I had a pillow in my hand. She grabbed at it in a fury.

There was only one tactic when this happened. I had to stand back and do and feel absolutely nothing until it subsided. It was very difficult not to let my feelings get hurt. When this fury rose in her, it was ungoverned and filled with dark power. All of us have such anger inside us but it's been socialized into submission and that's a good thing. Lissa's emotions were completely unrestrained. Finally, she subsided. The anger drained out of her.

"Where's Bert?"

Bert had been knocked on the floor.

"He jumped ship when you got so mad."

I picked Bert up and gave him to her. She kissed and hugged him.

"I'm sorry, Bert."

"What about me?"

She looked at me and couldn't remember what I was talking about. The anger was gone and as far as she was concerned, nothing had happened. Were I to cling to my hurt feelings, our visit would have been poisoned.

"What?"

"Nothing. So, what's the gym like?"

She thought hard. She was drawing a blank but then it all came to her. You could see it happen.

"Oh yeah. Karen. It's a big room. They have mats and machines and things. Some people are so hurt I don't know why they even try."

A tall, distinguished looking gentleman in a blue blazer and pressed slacks stopped in the doorway, looked at us, gave us a vague smile, a nod, and then he continued on his way. I went to the door and watched after him. He walked erect, purposefully down the hall, opened a door, went in, closed the door. I knew it was the linen closet. I waited. After a minute or so, he emerged, looked around and continued on his way. Everything about his appearance said success, competence, power, but he was a lost soul. Something had blown, some circuit within, and he no longer knew where he was, or what he was doing. I learned over time that he'd been a high-ranking officer in the Second World War, and that he was back there now in his mind, looking for his men. He'd fought in the gruesome campaign at Ortona, Italy. Most of his men were buried there. No one visited him.

If you were ambulatory at all, meals at the Rehab Centre were to be taken in the lunchroom. Lissa didn't think much of this policy at first. She was always a fan of "room service." It was a strange parade of the damaged that made its way down the hall each mealtime, some with walkers, some in wheelchairs, some on crutches. It took some talk to get Lissa to join it.

The lunchroom was an unlovely place, and these meals were far from being a social time. Most ate in silence, struggling with whatever pain attended them. Conversation was terse, halting, conducted in hushed tones. Sometimes, visitors, especially children, lightened the scene. But it was never inviting, and Lissa hardly ever went willingly. If she was adamant, I'd order a pizza and we'd stay in the room.

Big fun at the Rehab Centre was the super sports bathtub. Christa came in one evening and asked Lissa if she'd like a bath.

"Bath? I'd never get in the tub."

"You'll get into this one."

We got Lissa into her robe and wheeled to the tub room. This thing was a wonder. It sat high off the floor and had a door, like a sports car and a comfortable moulded bucket seat. There were echoes of Victorian times in the sleek fibreglass lines of the thing. It was big and comfortable and Lissa loved it. She could make the transfer from the wheelchair to the tub almost entirely by herself.

"I want one of these."

"Our house is too small. It would take up a whole room."

"I miss our house."

"Where is it?"

"Rose Bay?"

"Guess again."

"Oh . . . right . . . the Rose Bay Fallacy. Uh . . . Stonehurst?"

"That's right. I was talking to Dr. Joyce. She says I can take you home for the weekend."

"Oh . . . oh . . . "

She was still crying when Christa started washing her hair.

JUST OFF THE MOUTH OF ROAD BAY, Anguilla, was your basic vision of tropical perfection, Sandy Island. It had a dozen palm trees, a coral reef and under one of the palms, a little bar/restaurant run by one Neville Connor. Neville was ambitious, hardworking and smart. He had a big smile and looked like a West Indian Gilligan. He'd run his speedboat out to the island every morning with a few coolers full of beer and ice and some chicken legs and lobster. It was frequented by a couple of charter boats and anyone Neville could talk into a day trip. He had a firm grasp of marketing, and we were lucky to get to the island when we did. It got crowded.

We sailed out there one day and anchored off the reef. I dove on the anchor to make sure it was set, well clear of the coral and in deep sand. Then we took the dinghy in to the island. We were Neville's only customers that day, and life couldn't have been much sweeter. We worked out a price for a lobster lunch, circumnavigated the island on foot, which took fifteen minutes going slow, and then got out the snorkeling gear.

The reef was alive with fish and there was no surge on, so the water was crystal clear. Davey was new to snorkeling, and a little nervous about the creatures of the deep. He and I swam out to the reef after working out a system of signals. We'd hold hands and if he saw something that scared him, he'd give my hand a squeeze. If I gave him one squeeze back, that meant there was no danger. If I gave him two squeezes back, that meant we should surface and talk. If I gave him three squeezes, that meant, "Oh no, we're gonna die."

Thus armed, we swam into a small, living reef of incomparable beauty. Elkhorn coral, fan coral, brain coral – living coral then. Parrot fish, angel fish, sergeant majors and blue chromis, schools of jack and big-eyed squid. Shadows and light. The warm clear water. And then . . . a six-foot-long barracuda. Davey gave me a squeeze. I gave him one back. He squeezed again. I squeezed twice. We surfaced.

"Holy doodle, Tom, what's that big one?"

"Barracuda."

"He looks mean."

"He does, but they're pretty shy."

"Ok."

So we swam on. There was a nice-looking shell on the bottom. I took a few deep breaths and dove down to get it for Davey. It was about fifteen feet down. As I was reaching for it, I disturbed a huge ray that was lying hidden in the sand. When he moved, he scared the living bejesus out of me and I surfaced in an instant. My form accomplishing this was unorthodox. I didn't know you could jump like that under water. When I broke the surface, Davey was laughing.

"I guess we should have been holding hands, huh, Cap'n Tom?"

"I guess so, Davey. You could have saved me."

We swam back to the beach. Davey talked Lissa into going to the reef with him, and they scampered off, hand in hand. As Marty and I sat under the palms sipping Neville's cold beer, we'd hear peals of laughter coming from the reef every now and then.

"He's the luckiest five-year-old boy in the world," said Marty.

"He's more fun than the movies."

"He loves you guys."

"I can't even think of all this without him in it."

We sat and looked out at perfect tropical day. I could tell Marty was a little blue. He was a man used to being the leader of the band, and valued his independence. This situation, while it was perfect for Davey, chafed a little on Marty. No matter what, someday he'd need a vessel of his own.

"Figure we'll ever figure it out?" I said.

"Not much to figure. This is paradise, Tom. Don't worry when I get quiet."

Now Lissa and Davey were in the shallow water on their way back to the beach. It occurred to me that this was all pretty formative.

"Think he'll ever date anything but gorgeous blondes with great hair and . . . ?"

Lissa and Dave were in a serious splashing match. Marty considered my question in his thoughtful way.

"Blondes. He's marked. There's no hope for him. All of his loves will carry echoes of Lissa."

"He could suffer worse fates."

The two of them, dripping and alive, came running up the beach towards us, hand in hand, all full of love and sunshine.

"We saw the ray again, Tom. He's as big as a house."

"Davey said he scared your pants off."

"Where are those pants?"

And so the day passed. Neville barbecued the lobster and we ate them, with some good homemade slaw and buns. Then, as the shadows lengthened, we rowed back to *Avenger* and sailed her back to Road Bay. We dropped anchor as the sun set, and Marty got out his guitar and sang some beautiful old songs as I threw together a light supper for us all. We ate by lamp light, enjoyed another episode of "The Adventures."

"Snort, chortle, poop, Rats Crapskies!" In three part harmony.

"Black Magic Island loomed high and dark, belching a sulfurous cloud of ash and evil as *Avenger* and her stalwart crew clawed bravely towards Satan's Bight, the only anchorage in its steep black cliffs. The closer they got, the thicker the ash and the fiercer the foul-smelling wind. Gypsy Davey and Gypsy Daddy were on the bow, ready to drop the anchor when . . . "

We were in bed early that night, visions of the flaming festering bowels of Black Magic Island haunting us all.

25

AUTUMN IS A MAJESTIC AND MELANCHOLY TIME. The light grows clear, the shadows long, the air crisp and clean, the days ever shorter, and in a symphonic movement of colour, wind, rain and "the dying of the light," the soft and easy days depart. I love the season most of all. But since I moved aboard the schooner, fall has come to be the time when you're watching the sky and barometer, checking the weather for a window south. If you're not, there's a burden on your heart and soul. Winter, for all its glories, no longer holds much charm for me. *Avenger* doesn't like winter either. You can feel her pulling her shoulders into her ears. She loves the warm salty water of the Caribbean on her decks. Adds years to her life.

So we were comrades in adversity, she and I. She smelled of hardwood and coal smoke, and I smelled of rum. The careful reader will have noticed that I have a nodding acquaintance with rum. I do. I love the stuff. It is a noble spirit, the fruit of the cane, with the heat of the islands in its heart. Managed thoughtfully, it is a boon companion. There is danger there and you're wise to reef down when the rum squalls come too often. I would pass my evenings aboard writing, making songs, reading and talking to myself. Rum was the leavening, and my usual evening included three. Sometimes less, sometimes more. On the evening in question, there were more.

"I know you're hurt, old girl," I said to her. "You've got more cracked ribs than I do, and fifty thousand deep water miles under your keel and some of those were wild, weren't they? Jesus, they were wild. Don't know how we handled it. Good thing you're better than me."

You have to talk to your boat. Boats that no one talks to sink. They come apart at the seams. Violins, guitars, houses, they all come apart if no one talks to them. Other topics discussed that night will remain in the shadows. Boats will hear with equanimity things that cause agitation and alarm in most folks.

Once the fire had been burning for a while, and the boat was warm and dry, an uneasy peace settled over the night. Uneasy because the boat was in the ocean, and the ocean has ideas of its own about peace and tranquility, and how long it will carry such bliss. I went up on deck to look at the world. Despite its gentrified waterfront, Halifax is still a great old port. There was a brigantine called *Fair Jeanne* tied to the other side of the wharf waiting to go south. There was a big moon haloed by a big ring of light, a moon dog, and high clouds that scudded across the sky, promising wind.

"Oh, to be fully provisioned and bound for Anguilla." I gave *Avenger*'s mainmast a little hug, looked around the pretty new wharves. Not a soul in sight. The cold knifed through me and I went below.

I was worried about money. I'd been doing nothing but taking care of Lissa since the accident, except for those few days on the movie, and the kitty was low when it happened. I had to figure out a way to make some. Since I couldn't visit her until four at the Rehab, I had most of the day. So I made an album. I couldn't think of anything else to do, and I had a bunch of good songs that I'd never recorded. I called Georges Hébert, a fine guitar player and friend who had a good little

The schooner *Avenger* in the foreground
backed by the brigantine *Fair Jeanne*

studio in his basement. All he charged me for was the tape. I'd work on the songs on the boat after visiting Lissa, go to the studio in the morning and record two or three, and leave them with Georges. He'd lay in more guitar and then we'd talk about what else it might need. Bill Stevenson, Betty Belmore, Gordon Stobbe, Garth Proude, Skip Beckwith, and Janet Munson all offered their services. I still like to listen to *Clean Getaway* now and then. But I might as well have taken up farming for all the money it made.

The stimulation at the Rehabilitation Centre had precipitated a chaotic state in Lissa's head. She was starting to walk, learning to write, speak, cook, take care of herself, and was awash in fears and furies. They'd had her on tranquilizers since shortly after she woke up. There are fears about seizures and mood swings with head injuries and the pills seem to help. But when we tried to taper them off, the result was Yosemite Sam vs. The Tasmanian Devil, best out of three. Her memory was more vivid but completely out of control. One minute it was working, the next it was gone. It felt like three steps forward, two steps back or vice versa most days. I found it very difficult and so did Lissa. We wanted steady forward motion. We felt like we'd earned it. Expectations are the enemy. Better to deal with what's really going on. Especially when things are serious. Generally, that's when you're dealing with something provided by the fates and not something you thought up. Not that things you think up aren't a good and worthy part of life. It depends where they're coming from. I'm thankful for imagination. She's been a friend of mine.

It wasn't long before Lissa was wheeling herself around, and using one leg for speed. They'd pinned her name, floor and room number on the back of the wheelchair in case she forgot where she was. The scene at the centre was tragic and uplifting and full of human goodness. It was also, by times, funny. Bewildered souls would drift in and out of the scene, like something in a Marx Brothers movie. I'd wait by the elevator at four o'clock. The door would open, there she'd be, wheeling towards me crying.

"Always with the crying," I'd say like some Borscht Belt comedian.

"The pool! I was in the pool! I could move!"

This, while she was wheeling for her room like there was some kind of hurry. Once there, we had the usual debriefing about the day. Lissa struggled to remember all that she'd done, and it came at me in joyous bursts with forgetful moments in between that pissed her right off. Once we'd managed that part, there we were, two old friends and lovers together in one monstrous pickle.

"I'm sorry, Tom."

"We both are . . . about the bus. But this is all right, Lissa. It's hard but it's good."

"Where's Bert?"

"He's putting the blocks to Mini like he has been since the night they met."

"Constantly. Where does he get the energy?"

"And the chafe. I worry about the chafe."

Someone had brought a white, girlish-looking bear with boxing gloves. Lissa called her Mini, introduced her to Bert and the bears' arms entwined in an embrace that ennobled both of them.

"What about sex, Tom?"

"All in all, I think it's a good thing."

"But you're not getting any."

"Neither are you."

We looked at Bert and Mini, locked in their teddy bear ecstasy.

"You'd think they'd show a little restraint."

"You'd think."

~

THE REGGAE VERSIONS OF TIN PAN ALLEY carols heralded Christmas and Lissa needed to see her family. So we sailed back to St. Maarten. Marty and Davey tended the vessel and held down the gig at Pinochio's and we got on a plane. Oh, the shock of America when you've been living in the Islands. There's so much stuff! It's crazy. There's twenty-five of everything. Whether you need it or not. Beyond the avalanche of things, and a warm visit with Thelma, I remember only one evening from our time in Tennessee. We'd been invited to dinner at the country club by Lissa's cousin Mary Lawson and her husband Bill. Mary Lawson and Lissa were contemporaries. One had run away, one had played the game. Bill was a good old boy, a Viet Nam veteran who'd been set up in a beer distributorship by his father-in-law. He worked steady and made real good money.

They had a big new house, in a new neighbourhood. There was no dust, no clutter. Every hair on Mary Lawson's head had been carefully told where to go and every hair had behaved. Lissa had just picked up about four rolls of film that we'd taken in Nova Scotia and the Islands. We sat around their table, sipped bourbon from crystal and looked at the pictures. Bill kept saying,

"Goddamn . . . Goddamn . . . " and looking wistful.

The country club was faux Ante Bellum, but faux on a generous budget. The pillars may have been new, but they were big. We were greeted at the grand portal by the doorman, who whisked the car away as the maître d' invited us in and sat us in solitary splendour in the grand dining room, empty but for us, and a huge crystal chandelier twinkled electronically overhead. Bourbon and steaks were ordered. Lissa and Mary Lawson caught up on family. Bill and I worked at being good company. Something about the way we lived was gnawing at Bill.

"Ah got to say, Tom, Ah admire the way you just go ahead and do what you want," said Bill. "Ah never met anyone who just walked away from the world and went sailing."

"Well, the Islands are part of the world, Bill."

Mary Lawson could see danger in Bill's train of thought.

"Lissa, this is just a one year thing, isn't it? You'll settle down soon."

"Settle down to what?" Lissa was toying with Mary Lawson, aware that her suntanned presence was a challenge.

"You know, a house and job and kids. Real life."

"Our life is real. It's just different."

"But what do you do living on a boat?"

"We take care of the boat and each other, and when the mood strikes us, we raise the anchor and sail to another island."

"But you can't just sail around forever."

"Why not?"

We were having a lovely time. The steaks had been perfect, the bourbon was old, and the company congenial. Lissa and I were enjoying Mary Lawson and Bill's attempts to understand our life. We had been living outside convention for so long that we'd forgotten how radical it looked to those on the inside. Bill was like a dog with a bone.

"What about money?"

"Bill, I've always been a freelancer. If I need money, I write something, or get a singing gig. Or we charter the boat, take folks sailing. We don't need much, as long as we can afford the next haul."

"Haul?"

Lissa handled this one, and you should have seen Mary Lawson's eyes.

"We haul the boat out of the water twice a year and clean the bottom and paint it, and check that the caulking is still tight and replace the anodes. She's wood, so you have to be careful about teredo worms."

"You do that?" Mary Lawson was impressed.

"Lissa is a good sailor. She knows the boat and how to take care of her. The two of us can do a haul start to finish in four days."

"How did you get so . . . different?"

"Mary Lawson," said Lissa, "I always wanted out of here. I always knew there was more to life than shopping and keeping house. We used to talk about it when we were kids."

"Ah know we did, but talkin' about it and doin' it are two different things. All kids talk about going off on adventures. But you did it!"

"And the sky didn't fall."

"If one of my kids did what you're doing, Ah'd never be able to sleep, what with the worry."

Bill drained his bourbon, ordered another round. He was deep in thought.

"So," said Bill, serious, "what kind of insurance do you carry?"

"Not much. Just some liability in case anyone gets hurt on the boat. Hull and rig insurance is too expensive."

"Goddamn. You two are like the pioneers, livin' by your wits, takin' care of yourselves. Ah got to say, Ah admire that. Hell, Ah got so much insurance Ah almost wish somthin' bad would happen."

"Bill, how can you say that? You have to provide for your family."

"Ah know that, Mary Lawson. What Ah'm talkin' about is the way Tom and Lissa have got things down to followin' their own dreams. Ah mean, you get born, you go to school, join the Marines, come home, get married, work, have kids and die. There's got to be more to it than that."

Mary Lawson looked at Bill like he was from the moon. She'd never seen him confronted with questions like this. She struggled to offer him some comfort.

"Bill, you play golf. Maybe you'll get a hole in one."

Lissa and I flew back to the Islands and when we landed, we felt like we were coming home. The simple rhythms of life in the islands, buying fish from the fishermen, picking mangoes from the trees and sailing our home from nation to nation offered us time to think, to learn, to be. We felt a burden of guilt because we were from North America, and life as it is lived there is killing the planet. When you sail the Islands in a traditional schooner, and make friends whose lives are lived with such simplicity that money is almost unnecessary, you learn the depth of the madness of the first world and the depravity of the sacred bottom line.

26

ONE DAY, LISSA WHEELED INTO THE ROOM with nothing but a sidelong glance for me, parked her chair, and using her new cane, rose from the chair and went to the loo. This was not a demonstration for me. She needed to pee. I sat amazed, the toilet flushed and she walked into the room and sat on the bed.

"You walked."

"I almost peed my pants."

"You walked!"

"Karen gave me this cane. I have to do laps in the hall after supper."

"How long have you been able to walk?"

She thought for a while, looked at me, smiled that lopsided wonder of a smile.

"I can't remember. Not very long."

"This is great."

"I want to run, Tom."

"One triumph at a time."

As soon as she could walk, I started taking her home for weekends and holidays. I tried to show her as much of her old life as I could each time. I took her to the waterfront to see the boat.

"Oh Tom, I love her so much." And tears. Always a mountain freshet of tears.

"Remember *White Sails*?"

"Was she that colour?"

"She was green."

"Marty and Davey and Betty and Bill and . . . "

". . . Junior and Chris driving the van with the gear."

"It's all foggy and broken up. Did we have fun?"

"It was big fun, Lissa."

"I thought so."

I took her to the Lost Parrot in Chester. It was run by David and Sandra, who'd provisioned our first voyage from the back of their rusty pickup. The Parrot was one of a number of peerless joints that they had run on various frayed shoestrings over the years. It had been our favourite hangout. We walked in, Lissa on my arm, and made our way to the round table in the back. David saw Lissa, cleared the way and held her chair for her. Sandra stood, eyes wide and filling, her hands over her huge smile, making little laughs and snuffles. Lissa sat. David cradled her head in his big hands, kissed the crown of her head and wept for joy. Lissa reached up, held his arms.

"Oh . . . David . . . you old . . . I love you."

"I love you, Melissa."

Here is the wonder and deep importance of friendship. David and Sandra had given us corned beef and cabbages, pumpkins and potatoes and onions when they hardly knew us and these had sustained us on our voyage to the islands. We always loved their company and were soon to seek them out when we sailed home each summer. There had been dozens of alfresco banquets, help for one another in adversity. All of this was in the embrace David and Lissa shared. If you find yourself in such a hug, consider your life well lived.

I took her to Bill and Kerstin Gilkerson's beautiful home. Their golden retriever had delivered nine pups. We positioned

Melissa on the floor, her back to the couch, and then Kerstin released the pups, and nine fat furry golden balls of enthusiasm for the proposition that they were alive stampeded across the floor towards Lissa, who was calling to them with mad joy. She was swarmed. They nearly licked her to death as she laughed, great irresistible peals of laughter. It was a happy room in this vale of tears. That phrase, "vale of tears," is one of my favourite lessons from a Catholic schooling. They never let it out that the complete phrase was "vale of tears and laughter." There's your blockbuster. Lasts a lifetime . . . two intermissions.

I took her to Magnolia's Grill, the restaurant that she'd helped to create. After much fussing and hugging and such with Nancy and the rest of the staff, we settled into one of the booths and ordered some Cajun shrimp. After dinner, Lissa had to visit the loo. I took her, and noticed the eyes of the other patrons, wondering what to think, where to put their eyes as we hobbled along. It's a hard thing to look at someone who's been hurt bad. Perhaps it's because it's another forceful reminder of the fragility of life. But if you look deeper, if you see the courage and determination and lust for life in every faltering step, your eyes will soften and offer courage and affirmation to the hurt one. And this is how it should be.

I took her to the beach one blustery Saturday afternoon. We parked where we could see the water, and ate our sandwiches. I cracked the windows so we could hear the waves rolling in. It was brisk. Then I got her out of the car and we stumbled together across the jumble of egg-shaped granite stones to the sandy beach beyond. There we stood. The surf was up, and there was salt spray in the wind. Lissa hauled it in, deep inside. Over and over with deep gasps, she drank in the ocean, hungry for the salt and relentless power of it, a sailor home by the sea. We walked for a while, stopping to watch when the break was big. We saw a man and a dog far down the beach. The dog ran to greet us. When he saw the welcome in Lissa's eyes, he leapt up on her and kissed her face. I had to work to keep her on her feet.

By the time the man arrived, Lissa and the dog were chums.

"Sorry," said the man. "Usually, he's pretty well behaved."

"What's his name?" said Lissa.

"Barney."

"Barney, you're a big wuss." And she gave his ears another woolling and Barney and his human continued their rambles.

I took her home. Our house is tiny and very old. The local wisdom has its age at two hundred and fifty, give or take. Once, two families lived it its four tiny rooms downstairs and two up. Now its two down, two up, as we've tried to open things up a little. No one rich ever lived here. Its a humble fisherman's cottage. When I realized that Lissa would find it impossible to negotiate the stairs from the bedroom upstairs to the bathroom downstairs, I called Jim Rhodenizer, the best shipwright I know. We designed a "captain's bed" for the end of the long room, right next to the bathroom. Jim built it in with drawers and shelves and a desk for Lissa. It looks fine and works a treat. It's good to have the bed near the fire when the cold north wind is howling. The house has echoes of Carl Larsen's tiny perfect house in Sweden. Larsen had made a virtue of smallness and the house is the subject of a beautiful book, and a national treasure in his homeland.

The other room downstairs is a country kitchen. It's one of the best kitchens in the world. No kidding. It's been in *House and Home* to our great amusement. It's also been the scene of many a celebration, none more than Lissa's first dinner at home. Arthur, Susan, Bill and Kerstin came to dinner. Lissa sat at the head of the table and entertained her guests. I worked the galley like a mad fiend, chopping, peeling, searing, reducing. There were toasts and jokes and stories, and good food. Bill was writing a novel, and read the first chapter right to Lissa. She loved all of it.

"Clean your act up a little, Bill, and you might amount to something someday."

And peals of laughter. Her poker face was gone forever. But she may have been right. Bill trimmed his beard and the book did well.

I took her back to the Rehabilitation Centre. Each time we returned, it was more difficult. Yet I needed the rest her time there offered me. When she was home, every waking moment was consumed with care giving. This is a complicated thing, being the whole one taking care of the shattered one. There are resentments and confusions. Her calls to me – "Tom!" – so urgent, sometimes felt unkind and thoughtless to me. "Doesn't she know I exist, that I need some peace?" Her fears, while easy to understand, were difficult to bear. We had always been brave together. Now, while there was more courage evident than ever before no matter what the storm, in every waking moment there were also the fears. "I can't . . . no . . . it's too hard." I would grow angry and impatient and then hate myself for it.

She would grow resentful and angry with herself because she needed so much help. She hated her fears as much as I did and would try things that were beyond her. For her, every waking moment was a trial, every thought, every movement a triumph over adversity. Ten times a day, she would lose it, lose her sense of who she was, what she was doing, and sit bereft and bewildered, wondering what she could do to get it back. She looked so lost. I watched these battles, awed by the brave immortal spirit that compelled her to continue.

Often, on the drive back to Halifax, Lissa would decide that she wanted to have a joke ready for the nurses. We'd go through my inventory, find one we both liked and then I'd teach it to her. It was a matter of picking the right material. She couldn't do the long shaggy dog yarns I favour. She needed short, punchy stuff, easy to remember. For the life of me, I can't remember one now, but I do remember her delight when she got one right. In truth, she didn't need jokes. She was funny enough without them.

After we returned from our Christmas in Tennessee and the job ended in St. Maarten, we sailed to St. Barth's, where Marty found a boat to take care of and he and Davey moved aboard. We missed them, and often gathered for dinner and "The Adventures" aboard *Avenger*, but it was fun being alone on the boat. Our honeymoon at last. We sailed to Isle Fourche, anchored off the steep cliffs and swam and watched as two other wooden boats sailed in and anchored nearby. One had a wind-surfing basset hound named Pearl aboard. Pearl had long velvety ears and eyes filled with longing. There were shared meals, and exploring the island, which was inhabited by goats and iguanas. We snorkled. We read. We made love. And when the spirit moved us, we raised the sails, pointed the bowsprit at the next island, and so it was.

We sailed the boat well together, always carrying sail right to the anchor, and never a raised voice. There are those who'd see our life then as aimless and irresponsible. We were contributing nothing to the society that had raised us up, but we were also taking nothing away. We were on a voyage of discovery, learning that there are ways of looking at life that have little to do with first world notions of success. We fell into the soft music of the Islands, learned to treasure each day as it unfolded. Friends visited us from back home. We delighted in sharing what we'd found.

I took to this way of life more easily than Lissa. She had concerns about the future, about accomplishing something tangible in the world. This was not a persistent or difficult argument. It was just something we talked about.

"Could you really do this forever?"

"Probably. The thought of rejoining the rat race is scarier than finding myself an old fool in a leaky boat in some distant port of call."

"But you have talent. You should do something with it."

"There's pen and paper aboard."

"I just wonder. I mean, I love this but sometimes it seems aimless."

"Maybe aimless is better than dedicating yourself to aims that belittle the planet and provide nothing for the spirit."

"Tourism is gonna trash these islands. Then where do we go?"

"There's always the next island."

"I just think you have to stand and fight for something in your life, do something worthwhile."

"You're right, Lissa. This is my dream, and you've joined in with an open heart. I know it doesn't go as deep for you. But there's something wonderful about sailing this boat on the ocean. It feels so pure to me."

"I wish I didn't get seasick."

It was a discussion that came and went, depending upon the delights on offer. We had to make money, and were always looking for the next charter, or the next place for me to sing for our supper. When we had money in the bilge, we'd sail somewhere new, and live each day as it came. We were fond of the treasures we found on the beach.

27

At last, it was time to go home. Dr. Joyce sat me down in her office and tried to warn me about the difficulties to come.

"In a way, this was the easy part. Now it's all going to rest with you."

"Friends will help."

She smiled.

"Yes, they will. For about three months. Then they'll go back to their lives. Very few stay involved."

"Three months will be a help and I know there's some who'll stay."

"You can always bring her back here if it's too much, so you can have a rest."

"We'll be all right."

"Be careful, and make sure she exercises."

"I will. Thank you for all you've done for us. This is a healing place."

"Good luck."

One at a time, the nurses and staff said goodbye to Lissa, all of them writing notes in her "memory book." Her abundant humour and courage had made her a loved patient. Christa, who'd helped her pack her things and get ready to go, was last. She fiddled with Lissa's hair, after helping her get her coat on.

"You be good to Tom."

"I don't know why I should. He's just going to put me out in the barn with the animals."

They hugged, kissed.

"Don't worry, Christa," I said as we waited for the elevator. "We don't even have a barn."

"Yes we do," said Lissa. She was serious. It wasn't worth an argument. I meant to build one when we got the money.

The guy in the booth at the parking lot had been relaxed about the rules when I didn't have the money for a space. He came out of his booth to shake hands and say goodbye.

"Seen 'em come and go. Hope you two have some good luck for a change."

"Thanks. And thanks for understanding when . . . "

"Don't mention it." He stuck his head in the window to talk to Lissa.

"Be good to this fella."

"I don't know why. He's just gonna put me in the barn."

We drove away, side by side in a grey K-car. The days of big yellow vans, red pickup trucks and the sweet old diesel Mercedes were long behind us. We'd lost our tans and were bound for a tiny world. We'd wheeled up and down and around narrow winding island roads in rented Mokes and Deux Cheveaux. We'd driven the Algarve in a Mini, the west where tourists don't go, and feasted on charcoal-grilled squid and good red wine. We'd rolled through Tennessee, and along the Skyline Drive in the Blue Ridge Mountains with Hank Jr. on the radio and the windows rolled down. We were always on the go. No more.

Now we were looking at settling down. Lissa had wanted to settle down. It's one of the things that had been our undoing. But our present circumstances, you'll agree, would be an extreme method for getting one's way, and churlish to even impute to a wild spirit like Melissa. So, with the dear old CBC on the radio, we drove away from there. She'd arrived clinically dead in an ambulance. She left a new person, in a secondhand Dodge.

It was the end of February. There was snow in the woods but the roads were bare. I'd filled all the wood boxes and the refrigerator. Lissa's new bed waited for her, all made up with clean sheets. The house was clean and tidy, a state of affairs that wouldn't last long. I took exit ten off the 103 so that we could drive through Mahone Bay and along the shore in the afternoon light.

When we reached the turn off to our place, I looked at Lissa.

"You can cry now."

"Ok."

By the time we reached our driveway, I could barely see the road through my own tears. I pulled up in front of our tiny tumbledown house. Lissa looked at it all.

"I love this place so much."

"I hear the food's good."

I helped her into the house and got her settled. Then I brought her things in. She was delighted with her captain's bed, and set to work unpacking her things and filling the drawers. I'd set up the T.V. on the shelves at the foot of the bed. I turned it on for her, once we'd organized her stuff, and repaired to the kitchen. I was making Cajun meatloaf, a favourite of hers. As I put the meal together, she called to me with a thousand questions. For a while, I was happy to answer them, but as the cooking became more complicated, and the questions came closer together, I grew harried and had to fight the impulse to tell her to leave me alone. I prayed for patience, and it was provided. Desperate prayers like this I often send to my father. I do not believe that God meddles in our everyday lives, but somehow, prayers do get answered. I know this for sure. And if you need help with patience, read Job. Meditate. Deal with it. Patience is at a premium these days.

I set the table with candles and cut flowers in a blue vase, our best silver and prettiest plates, cloth napkins in napkin rings. I selected music for the meal that I knew she would love. Patsy Cline, the Temptations, Johnny Cash, Roy Orbison. When all was ready, I helped her into the kitchen, made her comfortable at the end of the table, and served the meal. We had begun our romance over a meal. Now, here we were again, and the feast rested on the same piece of wood, all that remained from the schoolhouse in Blueberry Bay. I poured the Beaujolais . . . raised my glass . . .

"Welcome home, Lissa."

"I'm sorry, Tom."

"That's not much of a toast."

"I'm sorry . . . "

This struck us funny, we laughed, clinked our glasses, sipped our wine and tucked into the meal. Lissa ate like a longshoreman, with many exclamations of approval. We had pears and cheese for dessert, and sat and talked and finished the wine. Then she wanted me to sing for her. I got my guitar, and sang a song I'd written for her to try to steal away a bad mood in Bequia, when the whole world was such a different place, and something as small as a humour failure could seem like trouble.

When I sang it for her on the boat in Admiralty Bay, the song had left her unimpressed, so dark was her mood. Now, it went through her. It went through both of us. She sat there, her eyes wide, and now and then, she'd mouth a few of the words. She was trying hard to remember. There were shards, random shells on the beach.

"Bequia. Was there a little hotel . . . ?"

"The Frangi. You'd pick up the mail there, in a little office with cubbyholes in the wall."

"Oh yes. There was a woman there, she was thin . . . "

"That's right."

"What was her name?"

"I don't remember."

"Was Doo Dah's in Bequia?"

"No. That was Anguilla."

And then, like a big wave had rolled in and washed away the shells, her memories faded and she grew sad.

"I can't remember, Tom. Will I ever remember?"

"I don't know, Lissa. Memory's a strange thing."

"But I loved Bequia, didn't I?"

"Yes."

"I wish I'd get better."

"You will."

"No. You shouldn't have brought me home. I'm no good. I can't think. I can't do anything."

"Don't . . . "

The grief poured out of her, her fears, her boundless sense of loss. All I could do was put the guitar back in its case, blow out the candles, and when she'd subsided, help her to her bed. She was well schooled in the rituals of getting ready for bed, and once they were begun, she became focused and peaceful. I left her to it, and returned to the kitchen to clean up. Standing at the sink, rinsing pots and pans, I fought the urge to cry. I lost the fight.

Refuse tears and you refuse love. Shed them too easily, and you make love less than it is. The story I struggle to tell you now was a lesson in love and compassion and hardship and courage and good humour and all that makes life worth the candle. But the memory fails and falters by times, and there's the rub. I write about an accident that destroyed Melissa's memory while certain my own is flawed. All I can promise you is that all of this happened to us, and these words are what memory provides.

Epilogue

FIVE CHAPTERS OF THIS were written aboard the *Avenger*, in the winter of 2003-04, in the Caribbean. For the last four or five winters, Lissa had been agitating for me to go sailing. She knew well how I ached for the sea. This was an act of selfless bravery. Though she is a complete human and full of virtues and wisdoms, she is hurt and needs help and I am her helpmate. And for her, sailing is no more. Last fall, there seemed to be enough money in the kitty to provide her with a qualified helper so that I could go.

One Saturday night, we sat at the table after dinner, listening to *Finkleman's 45*s on CBC Radio and talking. We were remembering sailing.

"Tom, you have to go. You've worked so hard on the boat. It's important and I won't let you stay one more winter."

"I think you're right, girl. I need a passage."

"I'm gonna give you a lot of shit on the phone about being Down South when I'm up here freezing my ass."

"I'd expect no less."

"Is Doo Dah still in Anguilla?"

"Doo Dah died last year. Beltoe's still there. He runs the place now."

There was a long pause. We listened to the vintage rock and roll.

"I'm gonna need a lot of presents."

"Lissa, no present money can buy or can match what you're giving me."

The passage was bliss, without storm or accident, and we sailed into Town Cut to welcoming smiles from ancient mariners. There were many blessings in my sojourn south. The most obvious was to be sailing again, to reclaim my body, my physical self and my old dreams. The most profound involved Marty and Gypsy Dave. Dave has become a professional sailor. He is tall and handsome and regarded as one of the good ones in the rarified world of mega-yacht sailors. His first command was *Whitehawk*, a hundred-foot wooden masterpiece with a reputation as a handful in every way.

I had expected that *Whitehawk* would be in St. George's when I arrived, and that Dave would see *Avenger* booming through the cut under full sail. We boomed, but he wasn't there. Maintenance and business had put his departure back. I waited as long as I could, the crew growing restive. I wanted to show him the boat. I'd rebuilt her over the last few years, with sweat and luck and brutal work and hope and prayers. She was looking good. Better than ever and every day, as I worked on her, I'd thought of Dave, and Marty and Lissa and I, and the strange family that we were, the passages we'd sailed together.

The day we were to leave for Antigua, I called Marty's home and found out he and Dave were a day out of Bermuda. I read the crew the riot act.

"I know you want to get going, but Gypsy Dave and Marty are going to sail through the cut tomorrow, and I'm going to be here and what happens after that is in the hands of the gods."

They were disappointed, but compliant. They had no choice. The next morning, as I worked in the galley, I heard his voice on the VHF. It was him. A man's voice, but his.

"Bermuda Harbour Radio, *Whitehawk*."

I listened to him talking, proud of how professional and self-possessed he sounded. Then, when he finished . . .

"*Whitehawk, Whitehawk* . . . Schooner *Avenger*."

"*Avenger* . . . *Whitehawk*. Hey, Captain Tom."

"Hey, Dave. When will you be in?"

"Be coming through the cut in an hour. Where are you? Over."

"Alongside, just at the turn before the gas station. Room here for you inside of us. I'll move off when you get in and then raft to you."

"Sounds real good, Captain Tom."

It was the way he said "Captain Tom." I sat at the chart table and pulled myself together. Then we got ready for *Whitehawk*. In exactly an hour, the majestic ketch powered through the cut under full sail. My heart was full beyond saying. Dave sailed her right up to *Avenger*, put her in the wind, and down came the sails. *Whitehawk* is huge, elegant and perfectly maintained, and there he stood at the big wheel, completely in command, doing it all with a nod and a wink. We moved off the stone quay, and Dave put *Whitehawk* alongside. Then we rafted up to him. Marty was with him. It was a glorious reunion.

The party raged on for days. The best part was always the late evening, sitting around the table in *Avenger*'s humble salon. There was always music. I'd never heard Dave sing and play. The night before we sailed together for Antigua, he asked for my guitar. After a couple of chords, the song began to sound familiar. And then, he sang it to me. "Island Folk." A song I'd written for *White Sails and Tall Tales*. He knew every word, every chord. It was part of his life. It was a song he sang often.

Most people live their lives without ever having such a valedictory. In that moment, with Marty watching, and everyone present aware that something rare was happening, I was given a gift that I will carry to the grave and with any luck beyond. When the song was finished, I grabbed my cell phone and called Lissa. I handed the phone to Dave.

"Hi Lissa. I was just singing to Captain Tom."

I won't try to write what he and Lissa said. Old love needs to be alone. When he finally gave the phone back to me, she was so proud, so happy, so sad, so full, so alive. I remember this about the conversation . . .

"Tom . . . is Davey good?"

"He's wonderful. Plays like Marty, sings like me."

"Well, one out of two ain't bad."

"You're wicked, Lissa."

"Don't you forget it."

We were bound down island to Bequia. It was blowing thirty to thirty-five every day. Getting ashore for provisions had been a job of work. I was eager to go. We rounded St. Maarten and pointed her for St. Kitts, with a deep reefed main, jumbo and jib, and we were in for a thrash. By now, I'd lost twenty-five pounds, gained a tan and some strength, and was one with the boat. I steered the whole way, til we got into the lee of St. Kitts, lashing the helm when I needed coffee, grub, or to navigate. My crew were young. Able, but young, and still becoming sailors, which both of them will be, to my great satisfaction.

It was lively out there, and every part of me was engaged in sailing that sweet old schooner, whose bones I have touched a thousand times. She was fine, and I had made her so. I thought of David Stevens and all that I had learned. Faces of every member of the standing crew of the schooner *Avenger* visited, smiled, laughed, ranted, and left as the sea hit her hard and she shuddered and surged on. My hand was light on the helm, easy and sure.

I don't know how anyone has fun with a boat they've only known for a year and mean to trade up in another. This year, after twenty-five years and fifty thousand miles, I learned things about *Avenger*, how she loves to go fast in a gale, how she needs no steering at all beyond correcting for irregular seas. I know her from truck to keel, and she knows me. Here resides the heart of love.

As we sailed along on that dark night, the schooner and I, Lissa seemed to be in the cockpit beside me, her brave spirit, her extravagant beauty, her willingness to leave the known world behind. It's a rare thing to find a partner who looks at the far horizon and is eager to go there, one equal to the demands of the adventure. We'd left the known world behind all right. And both of us had chafed at the lines that held us to the sure and certain demands of love: loyalty, compassion, forbearance, good humour and abdication of the self. After all the foolishness we'd managed when both of us were intact, we'd found the heart of love when one of us was shattered beyond repair.

In the beginning, it's all about beauty and promise and adventure and idealism and dash and style and victory. These are the loves of youth, and well suited they are to the times. But they hold too much sway nowadays. Too many songs carry the anger of youth, and too few the wisdom of age. As age gains a purchase, and experience teaches its relentless lessons, love moves with you and becomes its mature self. Love begins to cherish the known, the understood, the cared for and the well made, the trusted and the true. And at last unfolds the mystery, so huge at the beginning, so simple now. Why do we live?

Love.

Love comes home.

Photo credits

Chris Reardon – pages 8, 91, 104, 106, 132

Carl Sentner – pages 11, 20

Paul Toman – pages 21, 87, 111, 167

Tom Gallant – pages 26, 137, 159

Melissa Gallant – pages 99, 125, 156

Gerry Brimicombe – page 180

Rob Cohn – page 200